Learn How to Talk to Animals

A Practical Guide for a Magical Journey

Leta Worthington

Cover Design & Interior Typesetting: Hannah Levbarg

Cover image: French lithograph, artist unknown.
Used with permission of the owner, Leta Worthington

What People Are Saying...

Leta is the "real deal" on animal communication. I have consulted with Leta for my own animals and referred many clients. With Leta you get just what she hears from the animal and the information she gets makes perfect sense to the person who knows the animal best.

-Madalyn Ward, D.V.M.

Romeo is between 15 and 16 years of age, and has been in my life for eight years. He had many issues at first, but with lots of patience, love and Leta's guidance, Romeo was able to overcome his fears and became the most beautiful, confident dog. Leta was instrumental in assisting during a couple of life-threatening moments – without her help we probably would have been too late. Thanks, Leta!

-Elizabeth A, Houston TX

DEDICATION

I never could have learned what I now pass on to you, the reader, without the complete, unqualified and unconditional love and cooperation of my animal family. There have been so many in my lifetime, and every single one has played an important role. Just a few of the names that have come, and already gone, to whom I give great thanks: Spotty, Lance, Kittie-Wee, Ruggy, Circe, Petie, Sailor, Zak, Hank, Gabriel, Rose, Ferdinand, Ben, Theodore, Sunflower, Cutie Cat, Miriam, Moses, Fernando, Alice, Bessie, Keegan, R2D2, Pandora… and so many, many more.

And to those who are with me now: Sabrina, Bella, Corazon, Copper, Frida, Charlie, Bear, Tucker, Eloise, Sage, Lily, Kazumi, Mopsy, Lipton, and Mr. Smarty Pants and his Hen Harem.

CONTENTS

CONTENTS – CONT'D

PROLOGUE

My First Taste of Animal Communication

"Ha! This is a horse of a different color!" laughed Penelope. "He doesn't realize he's a horse, you know!" She then went on to say he had three bad habits: pushing, opening gates, and nipping—but reassured me that these were just baby behaviors and he would outgrow them.

Those words about my young colt, Sailor, were my introduction to animal communication back in 1985. I knew everything about my boy, from day one of his life, and Penelope's delightful and amusing summation of his personality and habits could not have been more accurate. I was flabbergasted!

This auspicious interlude in my life occurred while I was at a week-long horse training workshop in Palm Springs, California. The training method I was studying was new and innovative at the time, and dealt with things like "energy bodies" and "cellular memory" and "neuro-muscular reprogramming." Say what!? It was all a new world for me!

One evening during the workshop, over dinner in our condo, my suite mates and I were discussing our own horses and their particular problems. When I began describing Zak, my new hyperactive American Saddlebred, and some of the things about him that I didn't understand and that were problematic, Charlene piped up and blithely said, "Oh, you should call Penelope Smith in Northern California and get her to talk to him for you. She'll find out why he does all those things and it might help you figure out how to work him through them."

I was totally perplexed and asked, "What? You're kidding! How can she do that, especially if she's in Northern California and he's in Texas?"

"Oh, that's just what she does," she replied, as matter-of-factly as if Penelope were for hire washing windows. "She's an animal communicator, and it's telepathic, and she can talk to him from anywhere."

Now I was really in shock.

I continued to question and probe. Charlene had utilized Penelope's services not long before and described the experience in detail; plus Penelope's fee for performing this astounding long-distance feat was surprisingly reasonable (and she accepted credit cards). I decided to call Penelope right then and there. If you are at all familiar with the phenomenon known as animal communication, then you might know that Penelope Smith is perhaps the most noted forerunner of the practice in the United States, if not the world.

Although there are now hundreds of animal communication practitioners and teachers, she is still probably the best known in the field. Penelope was also the first person to formally train others to communicate with animals, and she has published several books on the subject. She still does extensive teaching and traveling but is no longer available for private telephone consultations. Back in 1985, however, she was still personally handling most of the calls that came her way.

I picked up the phone and dialed her number. Penelope herself answered! Still feeling overwhelmed by this new possibility and having no idea what to say or do, I simply answered her questions as we began:

What kind of horse was Zak?

How old was he?

How long had I had him?

What color was he and what did he look like?

And, the one that puzzled me most of all, where exactly was he right then (in a two-acre pasture on the western outskirts of Austin, Texas—how could that possibly help)?

As I was hesitantly asking her how she could find him from that measly bit of information, off she went, telling me all about Zak and why he acted the way he did. She also told me about certain traumatic incidents in his life before he came to me that had caused him to hold fear and anxiety.

It was a sad story, and she was very grave while relating it. But it all made perfect sense given Zak's behavior. Of course I had no way of knowing if these "facts" were correct or not. Still, the information made me feel I understood him much better and provided guidance in how I could help him.

Then I asked Penelope, "Well, while I have you on the phone, could you check in with another horse I have, Sailor, whom I've known since birth and have owned since eight months of age? He's two now."

"Of course," she replied. We went through the drill again, with me giving her Sailor's vital statistics and location. Before I could finish, she started laughing and said—I'll never forget her words—"Ha! This is a horse of a different color!"

Both Sailor and Zak were palominos, but I knew instantly what she meant, because never were there two more different personalities.

"Sailor doesn't realize he's a horse, you know. He doesn't understand why he's out there behind a fence and not inside with you, and he loves to entertain people and have them laugh at him. He's a clown, and he's extremely agile and athletic—he should have been a circus horse. What an imp!"

"That sure sounds like Sailor," I replied.

"He has three bad habits," she continued, still chuckling. "He likes to push you around with his body, he loves to figure out how to open gates, and he likes to try to nip you just to see if he can before you swat him away. He's not really trying to bite you, he's just trying to get a rise out of you. But don't worry, these are just baby behaviors and he'll outgrow them. You have to make it clear to him that some of these things are unacceptable and dangerous. I'll tell him that, but he won't quit doing them until he matures."

By this point I was speechless.

Everything Penelope had said about Sailor was true. She was laughing the whole time she was talking to him, so was definitely feeling his joyous, mischievous nature. Her report blew me away, and this was when I knew, for sure, that this woman was really tuned in and talking to my very own horses. I knew everything about Sailor from day one of his life, and she could have been connecting with no other horse.

In half an hour my whole world was turned upside down. I was so fortunate to reach Penelope when I did, for very soon after that she stopped doing individual consultations. One of her advanced students helped me with my animals several times over the next two or three years, and then I began my own study of animal communication. For a long time I felt like I was maybe getting through to the animals and that they were hearing me, but I wasn't sure I was hearing anything back. It was Sailor who provided the first real confirmation that I was on the right track with my studies, a few summers after Penelope had spoken with him.

I was working full-time and not doing much with my horses, so I arranged for Sailor to go spend a couple of months with some friends one summer. Although still his high-spirited, mischievous self, by this time he was five or six years old and trained to be ridden. My friends had a nice place in the country, another horse or two, and wanted him as an additional trail horse for a while. Plus, Sailor's half brother lived there and had a similar personality, so they understood Sailor's impishness. I conveyed the plan to Sailor several times, using all my newly acquired communication skills. I mentally showed him pictures of where he was going and assured him over and over in simple terms that he would enjoy himself and would return home soon. I described his outing as going to "summer camp."

When the day arrived to load him up and take him to his summer accommodations, Sailor absolutely refused to get into the horse trailer. Horses are often a little difficult to load, so we gave him some time and didn't push him too hard. But, since he had never had much trouble loading before, I couldn't figure out what was wrong.

I was standing about 40 feet behind Sailor so that my friend, who owned the trailer and loaded and hauled horses professionally, could handle him in her usual way, without my interference. After what seemed like forever, with my friend's fuse growing shorter by the minute, it dawned on me that Sailor had no idea where he was going or what was happening. He was not about to get into a strange trailer with someone he didn't know to be taken who-knew-where for who-knew-how-long or for who-knew-what-purpose.

"Sailor, it's time to go to summer camp!" I flashed to him mentally. "Remember what I've been telling you these past few weeks? Well today is the day, and if you don't get in the trailer you won't be able to go to camp. And I'll meet you there when you arrive." While sending him this "verbal" message I was also picturing and projecting visual images of where he was going and how much fun he was going to have.

Sailor turned his head all the way around and stared at me for about ten seconds. "Oh! Why didn't you say so," he said. Then he swung his head forward and literally jumped in the trailer!

That day's experience marks the moment I knew that even I could use animal communication successfully, and Sailor's immediate response lit my proverbial fuse and fired up my intention to fully pursue the discipline. Animal communication is for real and it really works. And you don't have to spend years learning it, like I did. You just have to want to do it and find a teacher and method that appeal to you. Meanwhile, I offer this book as a launching pad for your awesome journey and wish you great success and many blessings.

PART ONE

FACT OR FANTASY?

CHAPTER ONE

WHAT IS ANIMAL COMMUNICATION?

"Present and accounted for... let's get on with it!" snapped the aged Pekingese in a gruff, gravelly voice the first time I tuned into him. I was so shocked at this unexpected greeting—and especially at how it contrasted with his wagging tail and obvious excitement—that I started laughing out loud. I had been doing animal communication sessions for many years by this time but was still often surprised, amused, and delighted by the unexpected.

Animal communication is awe-inspiring, intriguing, sometimes a bit shocking (as in the above communiqué from our Pekingese friend), but almost *always* fun! Animal communication is, basically, a telepathic exchange or conversation between an animal and a person. Some think it is a psychic phenomenon, and that they would need superhuman skills to be able to do it. But, while a natural psychic ability might add a dimension to one's experience, one does not have to be a psychic to learn how to talk to animals. Anyone can do it if they want to and if they put their mind to it.

For many people, working with an animal communicator to get help with their animal companions is their very first experience with what might be called the "mystical." They are awed, intrigued, and sometimes a little frightened. But they almost always feel confirmed in what they already *"just knew"* about their animal companion beforehand, on their very own, with no one else's input or help. The animal communication experience often blows open their psychic doors and creates a feeling of being closely in touch with the Divine.

Most animals, on the other hand, seem to be familiar with the process and entertain quite comfortably the idea of speaking with their person— through someone else no less—mentally, in a "foreign" language, *and* from a remote distance. Although some may be a bit shy at first, many are downright matter-of-fact about the whole process and, like our little friend above, are often even impatient to begin the conversation.

So, no matter how you come at it—as a metaphysical experience or as an everyday event—dialoging with another species is pretty WOW, and thus begins a very special journey.

THE COLLECTIVE UNCONSCIOUS – WE ARE ALL ONE

Animal communication is actually only one form of what is called interspecies communication, which encompasses communication with the animal, plant, and mineral kingdoms on our planet, as well as otherworldly entities such as nature spirits, angels, aliens, and anything else imaginable that might exist according to each person's beliefs. Interspecies communication is very much in line with the theory that we are all one, and is a manifestation of the connection that binds us all. In shamanic traditions everything has intelligence and meaning—even inanimate objects—and a message or lesson to impart. Being able to tap into intelligence in all its forms is a divine gift we all possess at least to some degree—it is a birthright. In fact the great doctor, psychiatrist, and spiritualist Carl G. Jung described this mass of oneness as the "collective unconscious," and claimed that we are all, each and every one of us, a part of it.

This idea of oneness is parallel to what many people and sects proclaim—that we are all a part of God (the all-knowing that includes every aspect of consciousness, which goes by many names), and that God is within each of us. Jung included in his works extensive study of the unknowable, and in fact began using the term "synchronicity" to refer to meaningful or significant events or occurrences that happen without our knowing why or how. In other words, things that happen in our lives are not always explicable in the ways we might think they should be. Information comes to us from the collective unconscious—the all-knowing—through channels that we may not understand or be familiar with. We therefore categorize something like animal communication as a telepathic occurrence, something that happens through these unknowable channels—a phenomenon most of us are not very well acquainted with, are perhaps uncomfortable with, and certainly are not able to explain.

I remember my own first palpable awareness of what it meant to be part of a whole, or in oneness with others. I was at an advanced animal communication workshop where we were learning to talk to the wild kingdom of nature—animals and plants both included. (How this process is different from communicating with domesticated species is explained in Chapter 12.) For one of my exercises I connected with a type of low-growing grass that filled a wildlife grazing meadow. The meadow covered several acres, so there were thousands—probably millions—of individual grass blades, but when they answered my initial greeting and inquiry, it was as a whole. I was totally unprepared for the impact and sensation of having so many voices answer in unison, and as one, when I tuned into the meadow. There was a mutual understanding and intelligence in the grass of that field that so unified its individual blades, that, in that moment, I understood on a very deep level how the thoughts and actions of every individual influence and affect those of every other individual. I had read and studied about the concept of oneness for years, but it was not until I talked to the grass that I really internalized what it meant and what it felt like.

PSYCHIC VS. SCIENCE

Modern society has conditioned people away from using this natural gift of higher perception and communication, and for the last couple of centuries has focused on finding ways to scientifically explain everything we perceive and experience. As science has evolved, so has the belief that we should accept only those phenomena and conditions that can be proven through its methods. Add to that the fact that the Bible, which is a fairly recent rendition of *the way things are,* bestows upon mankind the position of "caretaker" of the animal kingdom, a treatise which, over time, has led to the belief that humans are superior to every other life form on earth because they supposedly have a higher intelligence. This certainly reinforces the idea, at least in Western cultures, that "truths" are acceptable only after undergoing scientific scrutiny. It has also fostered the belief that only human beings have souls, a premise that is discarded immediately when one starts talking to other species (and often by anyone who is close to an animal or feels connected to nature).

Not only do a lot of us humans feel superior, but we don't even consider many of the planet's kingdoms noteworthy enough to be categorized as "life." Rocks and minerals, which in shamanic traditions are understood to be repositories and keepers of special wisdom and power, are a good example of this. Another is the soil upon which we rely for growing our food. Although edible plants contain nutrients in direct correlation to the soil they are grown in, most people have no awareness of that soil as a living, organic, intelligent, and powerful part of life. Fortunately, as we move into a new age of enlightenment, more and more people are beginning to grasp the fact that *we* are not actually separate from *them*, whoever "*they*" may be—animal, plant, mineral, microorganism, or other. Talking to the animals is certainly nothing new. It has been accepted as a natural part of life on earth by many cultures and religions for tens of thousands of years.

SHIFTING FROM DUALITY TO UNITY

It is clear that a tremendous shift in spiritual consciousness has been occurring over the last several decades. We have left the 2000-year Piscean Age and entered the 2000-year Aquarian Age. Walk into any bookstore or browse online, and you can read all about this shift. In fact, if you are reading this book, you are probably aware of many facets of the *New Age* by now.

The Piscean Age was characterized by conflict and duality, whereas the Age of Aquarius, as the '60's song by that title so joyfully proclaims, ushers in "harmony and understanding, sympathy and trust abounding." This shift is bringing about a tremendous desire to reconnect with sources of wisdom and knowledge that exist outside the accepted paths and norms.

At the same time, there has been a resurgence of many of the old ways, ancient beliefs, and medicinal arts. The large number of acupuncturists, herbalists, Ayurvedic doctors, holistic veterinarians, homeopaths, Reiki therapists, and practitioners of other alternative healing modalities too numerous to list is a testament to the breadth of old and new traditions that coexist today. Alternative health practices are growing exponentially, because these techniques work. We are fortunate to be living in a time where we are able to avail ourselves of the miracles of modern medicine and at the same time plumb the depths of the wisdom of our elders.

This broadened recognition and practice of both the new and the old ways of healing extends way beyond the physical body and earnestly embraces the healing of the spirit, the soul, our planet, and consciousness in general. New ways of doing this that are appropriate to modern culture and science are developing. It is in this milieu that the modern form of what's called *animal communication* is developing.

ANIMAL COMMUNICATION & SPIRITUAL AWARENESS

I think it is safe to say that 99.9 percent of those who practice animal communication today consider it to be a spiritual endeavor and a healing service to those they assist. Talking to animals is a matter of the heart, and of *connecting* heart-to-heart when communicating. Techniques may vary, but healing the spirit and soothing both animal and human psyches through this heartfelt energy, as well as providing practical solutions, is what the animal communicator is all about.

Most animal communicators will affirm that mediating problems and helping human and animal companions connect goes far beyond simply using the tools and techniques at hand to conduct a conversation between two parties of different species. It requires extensive psychological awareness and sensitivity, finely honed mediation skills, diplomacy, and an opening of their own hearts to compassion and love. In essence, it is nothing less than a form of spiritual counseling. Any animal communication practitioner and/or teacher worth her salt is spiritually open and aware. She has also gained the ability to communicate and counsel effectively, not only through extensive study, but also through her own continuing personal growth and self-awareness.

I have packed this book with tools and techniques that will help you learn how to communicate with animals, and understand how functioning in a telepathic or psychic state is different from our regular, day-to-day mode. But the most important thing to remember is your intention, the love behind it, and the truth that when we operate from the heart, anything is possible.

CHAPTER TWO

HOW DOES ANIMAL COMMUNICATION WORK?

That is a big question, and it's one we animal communication practitioners and teachers hear often. Dr. Jung's theory of the collective unconscious becomes relevant here. If we are all connected as one energetically, then we all affect and understand each other on some level. Although that does not exactly spell out the intricacies of how unique individual entities communicate and understand each other through space and time, it is clear that they can and that they do.

How do you know when someone is angry? You might know because he comes stomping in the room, red in the face and yelling. Anyone can understand and relate to that. But how can you tell this same person is mad at you when you're on the phone with him, you can't see his face, and his tone of voice is perfectly normal? Aha. Now you get the idea. There is much more involved in telepathic communication than what you can see with your eyes, hear with your ears, or pick up through your other physical senses. When someone is angry, they project the energy vibrations of anger. If this person had walked into the room angry but was not red in the face or yelling, you would have still *felt* his anger. How do we pick up those energy vibrations and read them, especially at a distance?

ENERGY BODIES

We all have layers of energy bodies (also sometimes called "subtle," "etheric," or "auric" bodies or fields) that surround and extend beyond our physical body. Each of these correlates to some particular aspect of our being, i.e. mental or emotional.

Different disciplines identify these bodies in different ways, but they have been recognized as existing for thousands of years. They are as important to our essence as our physical bodies are, and in some ways perhaps even more so. They bear the brunt of trauma just like the physical body does. They shrink and expand in correlation to what we are emanating from our core, just as the physical body manifests health and illness. They can actually be photographed through Kirlian photography, and they change constantly, reflecting the state of our overall mental and physical health on a moment-to-moment basis. If they are damaged through an insult, injury, or emotional trauma, they need to be healed and sealed just like the physical body. They may even hold imprints of past-life experiences, which can then create health problems in the current lifetime. In fact, unless these traumas are addressed and healed on the etheric levels, the physical body will continue to reflect them indefinitely through health problems—possibly from lifetime to lifetime.

INTENTION

Some people can visually see auras, although most cannot. Children sometimes have this ability, but by the time they reach five to seven years of age—the so-called "age of reason"—they have had it conditioned out of them by being told repeatedly that such perceptions are "just their imagination." But we all have auras and are naturally able to perceive them in different ways, whether we realize it or not. Just as our inner being is reflected in our aura, so too can we project our energy vibrations outward… or expand our aura. How far and what we project depends upon how adept we are. It's logical, then, that energy projection is required for any telepathic or psychic experience. This is something we work on in animal communication classes and something one can learn to feel and control. Sending your energy out to another being is purely an act of will (intention), and will is the single strongest creative force in the Universe. Will is fire energy in one of its purest forms. Later in this book we'll give you some techniques to help you practice projecting your energy to other beings.

Once you have set your intention to do or to create something, honing your skills and practicing are the next steps. This is how you create your reality, and this is how you learn animal communication—through desire, intention, and practice (action). A good teacher helps but is not mandatory if you are able to focus clearly and follow whatever proven method you have chosen to follow. On the other hand, because of the spiritual and extremely personal nature of the work involved, a good mentor who can offer guidance and help you along the way is invaluable.

CHAPTER THREE

WHAT TO EXPECT IN AN
ANIMAL COMMUNICATION SESSION

These days, most animal communicators conduct their sessions by phone or, with the advent of the internet, by email, but also sometimes in person. If the appointment is by phone or email, you can work with any communicator of your choice, no matter where she is located, and most communicators do work long-distance.

Many communicators require a picture of your animal companion before the session, and some require payment up front. Some take credit cards, some use PayPal, and some may require a check before doing the session. Expect to pay what you would for a good qualified "people" counselor, but keep in mind that fees can vary greatly depending upon how the communicator works, how long she has been in practice, and what she includes in her rate.

Some may provide tapes or transcripts, or a follow-up, for example, in their fee, but some may not. Some communicators work evenings and weekends and some do not, so options for scheduling can also vary widely. Likewise, sometimes you can find a communicator who can help you out in an emergency right then and there. This usually depends simply on who you call, when you call, and pure luck.

Sessions may last anywhere from 15 minutes to two hours, depending upon the complexity of the case, how the session is conducted, and the experience, skill, and speed of the communicator. Many communicators have specialty areas as well, or may not work at all in certain areas (i.e. lost animal cases). As you can see, services and prices vary, so be sure you find the animal communicator who best suits your needs and budget.

Once you have decided to work with an animal communicator and have found the one who is right for you, there are three basic components you can expect in almost any consultation.

GENERAL PROCEDURE

I. GATHERING BACKGROUND INFORMATION

This usually includes a picture along with the animal's "vital statistics":

- Age

- Sex

- Breed

- How long the animal has been with you

- A description of why you are seeking the consultation, whether for health issues, behavior problems, or other reasons

- Important options you are considering, if any (i.e. re-homing the animal)

- Anything else that is pertinent to the case

II. THE ACTUAL COMMUNICATION

Again, this may be done by phone, email, or in person, with or without your direct involvement. The length of time spent in communication will depend upon the communicator's style and the complexity of the problem.

III. FEEDBACK AND FINE-TUNING

This is when the communicator conveys to you the results of the consultation she has had with your animal. This may be done by phone, in person, or in writing or email, and the form it takes can vary widely. Some communicators take notes and will give you a verbatim report on all that was said. Some will give you broad stroke information. Both are valid and, again, this depends upon the communicator's style and how she works.

In Chapter Thirteen, you can read a verbatim transcript of one of my telephone sessions. This was a communication done on behalf of a veterinarian whose young mule had bucked her off and is a good example of how in-depth we sometimes must go to fully understand a situation. It will also give you some idea of how the animal itself tells us "where to go next," or how to proceed during a session, in order to work through a problem effectively.

EXAMPLES OF WHEN ANIMAL COMMUNICATION CAN HELP

Animal communication can be effective in any situation where it might be helpful for an animal to understand what's going on. The following are just a few examples.

❖ You are going on a vacation or a long trip.

❖ You will be boarding an animal for some reason.

❖ There will be a pet sitter taking care of the animal, no matter what the reason.

❖ You are taking the animal to the vet.

❖ You are moving.

❖ There is any major event or trauma that affects you, your animal, or your family.

❖ You are expecting a child.

❖ You are considering introducing a new animal companion into the family, or you have already done so.

❖ There are important health issues requiring major medical attention or intervention.

❖ You must put your animal on a diet.

❖ You are taking the animal on a long trip with you. (Where? Why? When returning?)

❖ You would like to understand the animal's full opinion about something.

❖ Your animal is lost.

❖ There are life-and-death issues that need to be addressed concerning your animal, such as euthanasia.

❖ You would like to communicate with your animal's spirit after he/she has passed.

❖ You are leaving, for any reason (always tell your animal when you'll be back).

Once you begin practicing, talk to your animal about all kinds of things, certainly anything important. But if you feel unsure of your skill level, unclear or emotionally invested, or would just like an outside opinion, don't hesitate to seek the help of a professional animal communicator. Thirty minutes or an hour spent with such a person can do wonders to lift your spirits, help you and your animal companion find clarity, and encourage you both in almost any given situation.

CHAPTER FOUR

ANIMAL COMMUNICATION
ETHICS & RULES OF THE ROAD

You might be wondering, "If animal communication is such a God-given gift, everyone's birthright, an ability we all have, then why do ethics need to be considered? It seems like proper ethical considerations would be a natural part of the process." Well... some of us have a God-given talent for playing baseball, but that doesn't mean we're born knowing the rules of the game or what's expected from us as a third baseman. Likewise, we may need a little coaching in order to better understand our role as an animal communicator.

Most animal communicators would agree that using this gift requires not only compassion and empathy, but also discretion, diplomacy, tact, and skill. There are no acknowledged formal diplomas, degrees, registries, or certification levels for animal communicators and no established standards or guidelines. From where then do we pull a common moral thread on which to base our work?

Fortunately, in recent decades there have been wonderful pioneers in the field of animal communication whose work has trickled down, through print or their teachings, to help forge a common ethical and moral bond amongst practitioners. In fact, many of those originally trained by these leaders in consciousness have now published their own books and teach courses in animal communication themselves. The ethics of practice have been distilled and taught by many, but if you had to wrap them all up into one easy-to-understand idea that most communicators would agree upon, it might be something like this:

With loving care and compassion, animal communicators seek to encourage, support, and empower those they assist, thereby helping to create a unified spirit on earth through increased understanding between members of different species.

Doing this consistently requires great commitment and dedication, not only to the skills involved, which include diplomacy and counseling, language facility, intuitive awareness, and more, but also to one's self development. As you will read in the case of Jack the mule, in Chapter Thirteen, it is critical to be able to stay clear and unbiased in order to conduct a fair communication. We must therefore strive to continue to deepen our own spiritual awareness and growth in order to help open those doors for others. We must be willing to gather and present resources where needed—to educate, to get the word out, to walk our talk, and to speak our truth. Wrapped into these are other issues as well. As with physicians, clergy and counselors, animal communicators keep their clients' work private. We do not discuss our consultations with anyone or even acknowledge that they have occurred. We never, ever tread in territory where we are not qualified or where we may not operate legally by doing such things as making medical diagnoses based upon what an animal conveys to us. And we are always honest and up front with our clients about our own limitations and errors.

A few common desires are shared by most who learn animal communication. It would be fair to say that these people all love animals (often expressing a preference for them over humans), generally feel at home in and connected with nature, would like to help the animal kingdom in some way, and, by extension, help heal the planet. The base on which we stand is that "We are all One," a concept at the root of so many modern or revived belief systems today. We therefore honor one another and ourselves equally. Out of that flows a natural desire to ply our trade with compassion and caring, being highly sensitive to the needs of those we serve.

HONOR, RESPECT, AND REVERENCE FOR ALL LIFE

There is one area in particular that people are always curious about when they are learning how to communicate with animals. Invariably they will ask, "Don't you just go around talking to the animals all around you every day once you learn how to do it?" The answer is simple and clear. No, you do not. It's fine if you want to do this with your own animal companions, but ethically it is not recommended that you communicate with animals who "belong" to others without being invited to do so.

According to the Bible and many other spiritual traditions, one of the duties of humans on earth is to be the caretakers of the other species that abide here. Unfortunately, what was originally a divine directive has, through the ages, morphed into humans feeling far superior to all other life, so we now buy and sell—"own"—animals as freely as we do cars. To some, therefore, animals are part of their property or territory, and trespassing is not allowed. There are even laws pertaining to animals as property, i.e. it is still a felony to steal a cow or horse. (Please note here that when I use the word "owner" in this book, it is only in keeping with our culture's legal precepts and does not reflect my own personal concept of the relationship between human and animal.)

Since honor, respect, and reverence for all life are key tenets in the animal communicator's belief system, it is inherent that we must then also respect societal traditions and laws and operate within those bounds. A primary reason then that we do not talk freely to another person's animal companion without his or her permission is simple: we respect that person's privacy.

Another very important reason not to engage in depth with another person's animal is that we have no authority to influence change for that animal unless given permission. The following is an example that helps illustrate this ethical point.

THE CASE OF THE FRUSTRATED FARRIER

A few years ago I taught a three-day workshop in Oklahoma where 14 women and one man, a horseshoer, attended—Hans, we'll call him. Not surprisingly, being the only male in the group, Hans felt a little anxious and out of place, so didn't speak up much during the first day or so. He also heavily doubted his ability to talk to the animals and that what he was receiving from them was "real." But as the group grew more unified, and it became more and more apparent that his classmates were having success in their communications, Hans started loosening up. Finally, on the third day, as we began a discussion of ethics, Hans broke down and told us the real reason he had signed up for this workshop.

Hans couldn't hold it in any longer—he told us he had thought he was losing his mind before coming to my class. Several of his clients (the horses, not the humans) had started "talking" to him while he was working on their feet! In plain English! Now this man was from Scandinavia, so English was not even his first language. Perhaps he grew up with more open-mindedness than some of his Oklahoma counterparts, but in any case, he was sure able to hear horses talk—in English—at this point in his career. This had been going on for months, and Hans was becoming a nervous wreck. He not only doubted himself, he didn't have a clue as to what to do or how to reply to the horses. And, one horse in particular was giving him some pretty specific information about things happening in her life that bordered on neglect and abuse. Poor Hans was a basket case by the time he attended the workshop, what with his confusion over "hearing voices" from horses, his emotions over this one horse's plight, and his quandary about what to do or even if he could or should do something.

Hans' story is a good example of the kind of thing that can happen to an animal communicator (or to anyone, for that matter) and is a situation that has to be handled with great care, diplomacy, and skill. For Hans we worked out an acceptable solution and approach for how to respond to the horses who were talking to him uninvited. Wherever possible, he would relay any information he'd gotten that might be helpful to the horse's owner—say, a suggested change in diet a horse had proposed, or the possibility that the horse's feet might be sore from shoes that were too tight. Obviously, how and when—and even whether—he conveyed this information would be dictated by many things: the information he had received, the general receptiveness of the horse's owner to advice of any kind, and Hans' judgment of what was the best way to proceed in each case.

EXCEPTIONS

Casual greetings such as "Hello!" and "How are you?" are always fine to exchange with any animal. We animal lovers do that out loud, silently, and through body language all the time with both our own animal companions and those of friends, and even those in nearby parked cars. These are the same kind of casual exchanges that we might have with human strangers and are perfectly acceptable in the animal communication world. But entering into an in-depth discussion with an animal without its owner's permission is where a line must be drawn. Again, this is out of respect for privacy *and*, as importantly, because more often than not we are not in a position to do anything to help should a problem be brought to our attention.

If an animal persists in talking to you, as in the case cited above, one thing you can always do is tell the animal that you hear them, respect them, honor and love them as a divine being, that you acknowledge their problem and their pain, and that you hope it will be resolved. Then let them know that you are not in a position to help them in this situation, but if that changes you will certainly pass on their information and try to help find a resolution. If done with loving care, this simple acknowledgement in and of itself can do wonders to ease an animal's distress. Being heard is important to all of us—animals and humans alike.

Being willing participants in the evolutionary struggles that go on upon this planet, domesticated companion animals are generally very aware of the concept and strictures of "ownership" in our society. And they are usually as attached to their owners as their owners are to them, so, under most circumstances, are quite able to go along with whatever decisions their owners make for them, and indeed sometimes sacrifice their own lives for that person. Still, they do appreciate a sympathetic ear.

The blanket exception to the "must-have-permission" rule is that you may intervene and do whatever you need to do in a life-or-death situation, with or without permission. You may rescue anybody's cat from a burning building. You may bodily pull a dog away from being severely beaten, just as you would any child or human. In these situations you must use your judgment and follow your heart.

If you decide to learn or practice animal communication, and you're coming from a place of kind intention and loving compassion, staying within the ethical "rules of the road" should not be a problem.

CHAPTER FIVE

STAYING OBJECTIVE AND USING GOOD SENSE

Animal communicators are simply "messengers." We are here to serve as a link between human beings and their fuzzy, furry, feathered, and scaled earthmates—to bridge the gaps in understanding that naturally occur amongst species when they are unable to read each other's desires, feelings, thoughts, and spiritual essence. During an animal communication session we go back and forth between companions, human and animal, allowing each of them to gain a deeper understanding of the other. It is not our role to interpret subjectively or psychoanalyze what is going on; we are here to translate, to convey, to carry the subjects' messages back and forth, and to help mediate and mitigate, if possible, any difficulties that may exist.

Sounds simple, huh? It can be, but sometimes it can also get tricky, especially since our own opinions and judgments have a way of sneaking into the picture.

There are myriad ways of sending and receiving communications to and from other beings, most of which are employed singly or in combination, at one time or another, by animal communicators. The communicator is usually not even consciously in charge of how she is

receiving, and may get hit with a whole mishmash of different types of information at once. Now just *what* is one to do with that variety of information when very little of it is in a language that its intended recipient will understand? *Translate, interpret, describe, quote, convey, sing, dance...* whatever is required to get the message across.

REMAINING OPEN AND DETACHED

Here's a silly, made-up scenario to help you better understand why it's important to keep your communications free of your own opinions. Imagine that you are facilitating a discussion between a Bushman and his tribal bull elephant. The bull elephant keeps showing you a picture of himself pulling a large tree up by the roots, turning it upside down and shaking it. What does that mean to you? Nothing. What do you tell the Bushman (assuming of course that you speak "Bushman")? You very carefully describe the picture the elephant has shown you. The Bushman shakes his head. He doesn't understand. You ask the elephant again, and he shows you the same picture. Back to the Bushman—nothing. You ask the elephant again, but this time you ask him if he could please give you a little more information because this Bushman over here is just not getting it. So the elephant shows you the same picture, but this time there are nuts falling out of the tree when he shakes it. You convey this new image to the Bushman, and—aha! The Bushman knows exactly what this means and what he's supposed to do. He is to take his elephant and his tribe to the nut trees to the south and get those nuts harvested!

This absurd example is to give you an idea of how crucial it is that you form no judgments as to what is being relayed between parties, or, if you can't help but have a few in the back of your mind (like, "Jeepers, I think this elephant is about to destroy this bushman's village with this tree!"), you don't let them influence your discussion. Period.

TRUSTING YOUR JUDGMENT

Another story illustrates how important it can sometimes be to relay what you have heard an animal say, even when you didn't invite it and are hesitant to follow through.

THE CASE OF THE HORSE WHO WOULD NOT SHUT UP

One of my friends, Carol, had an injured horse and was spending her winter evenings after work at the stable where the horse was boarded. By the time she arrived everyone else had usually left, and she was there for quite a while because she had to soak the horse's foot in a bucket of medicated water. Another horse in a nearby stall began telling her, night after night, "I can't breathe! I can't breathe!" Carol had studied animal communication and was quite gifted, but she knew the rules of the road dictated that she not try to enter into a probing conversation with this other horse. She could sense and feel, however, a blockage in the horse's throat. This went on for some time, and the gelding would not let up in his plea to her for help. That combined with the fact that the client knew the horse's training was suffering because he got winded quickly, finally convinced her to approach the horse's owner and relate what she had heard and felt. She knew it would not be well-received, as this person was not open to animal communication, or to alternative medicine, and didn't even particularly care for my friend. But Carol braved on, related what she had heard from the gelding, and suggested it might not hurt to have his throat "scoped" just to make sure there was no blockage there. The gelding's owner huffed and puffed and defiantly stalked away. Sure enough, however, a week or so later out came the vet, who scoped the gelding and discovered a large benign, operable tumor blocking his air passage. Surgery was done, and the horse recovered beautifully and went back into training.

The moral of the story? Follow the *rules of the road*, but use your best judgment when faced with exceptional circumstances like these.

WHEN NOT TO USE ANIMAL COMMUNICATION

Whatever mode is employed or "translation" given, it is absolutely essential that our own opinions and feelings not enter into these interpretations. Offering our own opinions and feelings is appropriate *only* if and when the client asks for our subjective help, opinion, and advice. Therefore, it is wise not to practice animal communication when:

- you are not clear enough emotionally to be objective;
- you already have a very strong opinion about the situation and what the outcome should be for the animal involved;
- the animal lets you know in any way that he/she does not welcome your invitation to communicate (never push);

- you do not have permission from the animal's person to talk to their animal; or

- you intuitively feel, for any reason, that it is not a good time or a wise thing to do. Trust yourself here!

PART TWO

JUST DO IT!

CHAPTER SIX

GETTING STARTED

When we engage in a psychic or telepathic activity, we use active and passive abilities that we don't consciously employ in normal, everyday life. These abilities, skills, tools, or whatever you want to call them, are actually always at work within us to a greater or lesser degree, but we tend to dismiss most of the information that comes through these channels (like a sudden knowingness or intuition), if we even notice them at all. Our society rather flippantly lumps this entire collection of phenomena under what it may call the "sixth sense." A common attitude is that anything that can't be explained—seen the with eyes, heard with the ears, or otherwise physically perceived—must not be very important or legitimate.

How We Use Our Brain in Animal Communication

The human brain operates in many different energetic modes and at varying frequencies. It does not emit the same patterns of energy in sleep that it does during wakefulness, for instance. Likewise, there are some areas of the brain that function instinctively and others that function cognitively. Without getting too technical, it is important to note that certain states of consciousness are more conducive to particular types of activity than others. The speed and pattern of brainwaves vary, depending upon what state we are in. These different brainwave patterns can be scientifically recorded and documented for diagnostic purposes or for specific types of testing (such as lie detection), and it is widely acknowledged that brainwave patterns are integrally related to emotional states, behaviors and abilities.

One common way of identifying different types of brain activity is by lumping those activities under "left brain" or "right brain" functionality. Left-brain function is characterized by a brainwave pattern called "Beta" and is associated with cognitive skills like mathematics and technical thinking. Right-brain function, on the other hand, is associated with creativity and pursuits like painting and creative writing. As you will see below, learning to use both sides of the brain equally well is a very important aspect of animal communication.

BETA

Most of us go through our days clicking along in what is known as a Beta brainwave. This is the one we use to think cognitively, figure things out, do math, or tell our boss off in our head. It's the brainwave of mental activity, and the place where most people in this culture "live."

When we lie down at night to go to sleep, our brains go through a progression of patterns, from Beta, to Alpha, to Theta, and then to Delta when we are fully asleep. The patterns may vary in the night, depending on sleep cycles, but this is the general sequence when we "drop off."

ALPHA

Let's examine these brainwave states and see why they're important to animal communication. We've already talked about the Beta state— the workaday world, here-and-now, focused mental condition. Let's say you're rocking along in Beta mode one day when, while shopping on your lunch hour, you come across one of those chair massage opportunities. You know the one: 20 minutes for $20, you keep all your clothes on and sit up, comfortably leaning forward into a padded chair while some fabulously beautiful person massages your upper back and neck and transports you to Nirvana for half an hour or so. You get up and feel like you are floating on a cloud. Tada! You have just gone from a Beta state of consciousness to Alpha, perhaps even slipping a bit into Theta if you felt you were falling asleep. This is the nature of Alpha, which is the next level of relaxation down from Beta (or shall we say the *first* level of relaxation, since Beta means you're alert and not particularly relaxed at all).

An Alpha state of consciousness is relaxed, dreamy, open-minded, not obsessing about anything, and is generally a very pleasant place to be. Nirvana! If you have been resisting your spouse's buying a new little red sports car for months and then he or she catches you at just the right moment—in a blissed-out Alpha state—you might just be inclined to go for that little red car yourself! Everything seems easier when you're in this state. Life is good. This is also the state conducive to creativity, art, beauty and ideas. We are more suggestible in this state and we can more easily absorb new ideas (like little red sports cars).

We humans don't spend a lot of time in Alpha mode, at least not unless we're in bed, in a hammock, or sunning ourselves on the beach. In fact, we are usually thinking about things like work deadlines, the grocery shopping, or our bank balance. If you switch to Alpha while in your normal day-to-day routine, you may even find yourself feeling a little dizzy or woozy all of a sudden. You know how ungrounded you feel sometimes when you get up after that massage? Kind of loopy and light-headed? That's a common sensation associated with the Alpha state when you're not used to it. Feeling that way when you don't expect it and don't know why it's happening can be disconcerting and can even make you nauseous. It happens because you are not used to being in Alpha except in relaxed situations (for instance, at bedtime).

You can get used to functioning well in the Alpha state of consciousness, and this is an integral part of doing something like animal communication. Once you get used to shifting into Alpha, the shift will start happening easily, quickly, and unconsciously. You must be able to drop out of the physical world as you know it and enter another world where things are not perceived in the same way. To enter that world, you must be able to relax and change your state of consciousness while remaining in touch with your physical surroundings—a perfect Alpha state.

THETA

Theta is the next deeper state of consciousness before sleep, and is kind of a twilight zone. It is not a state where you could be actively up and about—unless you're sleepwalking. You might even have a realization that you are "asleep but awake" or "awake but asleep" at the same time while in this state. This is the level of awareness where people often see ghosts at night, hear someone speak to them audibly, or wake up all of sudden because they feel a cat who is deceased jump up on the bed.

This is truly one of the most fertile states of consciousness in which to receive brilliant enlightenment and new ideas. You may not register them on a conscious level until much later, but once they are implanted in your psyche they begin to germinate. This is also a time where you can enter the "lucid" or "conscious" dreaming state, where you actually know you are dreaming and take control, often orchestrating what happens next.

DELTA

From Theta you dive down into Delta and go into deep sleep. Delta is a very slow, long brainwave and, while much happens during our deepest sleep, including the dream life and out-of-body travel, this state is not relevant to animal communication as addressed in this book.

SHIFTING FROM BETA TO ALPHA BRAINWAVES

To hone your psychic or telepathic skills, it is very helpful to learn how to shift between the different brainwave states so you can become more receptive or responsive, depending on need, in any given situation. That's why most animal communication classes include activities and exercises designed to take students out of Beta and into Alpha. This can be done through meditation, guided visualization, and other exercises. There are also forms of music or drumming that are helpful for inducing certain brainwave states, and sometimes those are used as well. These exercises may not be identified with brainwave patterns (formally learning about Alpha and Beta states is not required or necessary)—they are simply geared to help one move into a more relaxed, receptive state of mind. And you don't need to be accomplished at meditation to shift into this relaxed state. It's easier than you think.

As stated above, because most people are not used to functioning in Alpha while they're up and moving around, they commonly have dizziness or nausea when they first begin experiencing Alpha under these circumstances. For this reason, when I begin training students for animal communication work, I have them alternate between right-brain and left-brain activities. This not only gives them some time to get used to a relaxed and receptive state of consciousness (Alpha), but also to experience what it feels like to function well while both halves of their brain are truly integrated. We live in a left-brained (Beta) world, but we can learn to use our right brain equally to have a more balanced overall connection with everything around us.

Some people have a harder time than others simultaneously using, or integrating, the two halves of their brain, but being able to do so is a must for animal communicators. To help get you started in this effort, practice the exercises below. These have the effect of firing electrical impulses in both sides of the brain simultaneously and will help you be able to shift more easily into the receptive frame of mind that is optimal for communicating telepathically.

BRAIN EXERCISE I – CROSS CRAWLING

When babies learn to crawl, they use a pattern called cross crawling, which means they bring opposite arms and legs forward at the same time. Their left hand will strike the ground at the same time as their right knee, and vice versa. This basic step in a child's development is actually one of the most critical in terms of enabling the child to use both halves of his or her brain. In fact, children who miss this critical developmental step, perhaps due to a physical impediment or abnormality, often exhibit other development difficulties as they grow. To cross crawl:

1. Get down on the ground on your hands and knees.

2. Begin crawling by bringing your left hand and right knee forward at the same time. Make sure both of these strike the ground at the same time.

3. Next, bring your right hand and left knee forward at the same time, again making sure that they strike the ground simultaneously.

4. Continue crawling forward step by step, focusing on striking the ground simultaneously with opposite hand/knee pairs. Keep your neck straight and your face parallel to the floor.

> 5. Crawl for up to five minutes to really reconnect the two sides of your brain. It doesn't matter which hand and knee you start with, just make sure to use opposites.

BRAIN EXERCISE II – MODIFIED CROSS CRAWLING

If you don't want to get down on the ground and actually crawl around, another way to create the same effect is with this modified method (it doesn't matter which side of the body you start with).

> 1. Stand in a relaxed but balanced position, with your feet shoulder width apart and your hands relaxed at your side.
>
> 2. Bring up your right knee and slap it with your left hand. Return to your starting position.
>
> 3. Bring up your left knee and slap it with your right hand.
>
> 4. Continue to alternate back and forth for a few minutes.
>
> 5. The sensation of your hand striking your knee will create an effect similar to the one achieved by cross crawling.

BRAIN EXERCISE III – USING YOUR OPPOSITE HAND

Another simple way to use and integrate both sides of your brain is to use your less-dominant hand to perform daily tasks. For instance, if you're right-handed and you usually open doors, brush your teeth, or point with your right hand, try doing those things with your left hand. Open doors, reach for objects, and even write with your left hand. Also, notice how you cross your arms or clasp your hands, and consciously switch to using the opposite pattern (right and left handed people have different patterns for these things). The more you use the less-dominant side of your body for routine tasks, the more you will activate and awaken the "sleeping" or more dormant side of your brain and facilitate a balanced integration of your right brain and your left brain.

Believe it or not, some adults find these exercises almost impossible to do on the first try. That is because they have been operating in one mode so predominantly that the other half of their brain is more or less "turned off" and has to be reactivated. Most people in Western cultures are left-brain dominant because of the types of activities and learning those cultures emphasize.

Play with these exercises as often as you can. The more you practice, the more integrated and balanced your brain will become. After even just a few hours of altering your brainwaves in this way and using new and different patterns of functioning, it will be much easier to move into practicing telepathy.

CHAPTER SEVEN

THE ANIMAL'S POINT OF VIEW

Most domesticated animals are not only open to communicating with humans, but are eager to do so. Even so, it is important to introduce yourself to the animal and tell him or her who you are and why you've come. It is also appropriate to let the animal know that you are making contact at the request of the animal's owner, so in essence are speaking for the animal's human friend. Once this is emphasized, even a shy animal or one who might be reticent at first, will usually warm up and willingly enter into a conversation.

Sometimes animals are surprised the first time a communicator tunes into them, but they usually relax fairly quickly and often become quite excited about the interplay. Most participate wholeheartedly. In fact, many of them will tell you that they communicate with their people all the time and can read just about everything in their minds. So for many animals, communicating telepathically in this way is nothing new. (They may however add that this isn't necessarily a two-way street—that often their people don't seem to understand *them* at all—and some animals think this is pretty funny!)

UNDERSTANDING OUR DIFFERENCES

It is essential to approach an animal with great respect and to let them feel and know that you honor them as an equal being. Each species has qualities, characteristics, and attributes which we may not understand, but which are valuable and unique to their kind—often for survival. Such unique characteristics and needs shape each species' behavior and habits.

We must not assume that, just because we can establish a free-flowing communication with an animal, we can reason away problems or easily talk them into whatever we want. Our ways are just as strange to them as some of theirs may be to us, and trying to override innate, instinctive behaviors or traits isn't fair and usually can't be done to any significant degree anyway. The following is an example of what I'm talking about.

THE CASE OF THE FAIRY-DOG, WINSTON

Several years ago, one of my clients adopted a tiny and delightful toy male fox terrier. In his babyhood, Winston came across as a spritely little nature spirit, and indeed, shared with us that he had never been incarnate on the earth before. Being a dog of any type felt very foreign to him—he himself, he told us, felt more like a fairy. For this reason we felt it might not be necessary to neuter Winston, and for quite a long time he did not exhibit any problematic or macho male dog behaviors. As he grew a little older, this naivete was still very much present in Winston, and he expressed to us that his intact state was a basic part of his essence and should not be messed with. We agreed.

But sure enough, as Winston matured into a full-grown, mature and masculine version of his toy terrier self, he also developed some of what we humans might consider to be "undesirable" behaviors typical of an unaltered male of his species and breed. Terriers are smart, curious, and lively, but they can also be fiercely protective and territorial. Winston developed these traits to the extreme, so much so that he began exhibiting strong aggression toward any other dog that came near his territory, and he began marking in the house!

After two or three sessions where we tried reasoning with Winston, and after working with remedies for modifying aggression, Winston's owner had to make the choice for him. Winston was neutered so that his hormones would not continue to bring out the fiercer, more destructive side of his feisty personality and breed. Fortunately, neutering did not quell the light-hearted, fairy-like part of Winston's personality, and he soon returned to his delightful self.

This is a good example of how we cannot just reason away instinctive behaviors. We could have talked ourselves blue in the face with Winston, explaining to him why he should not be aggressive with other dogs or mark in the house, and it would not have made one bit of difference because genetically he was predisposed to exercise these behaviors, just as any successful alpha male ancestor of his breed would have before him. Although in this case intervention was necessary, it was done with loving compassion as well as with Winston's knowledge and cooperation, so the outcome was positive for all concerned.

The more open you are to accepting each animal for exactly who he or she is, the more naturally you will be able to understand and communicate with them. This involves more than just setting aside personal or societal opinions about the animal or its species. It involves opening yourself and your heart so fully that you can really appreciate the animal's essence—and that essence may be a surprising combination of genetics and personality. An excellent way to get closer in this respect is to experience what an animal experiences, perhaps even through its eyes and other senses. To practice getting into the animal's point of view, work with the exercise below.

MEDITATION: GETTING INTO THE ANIMAL'S POINT OF VIEW

This exercise will help you actually experience what it feels like to be an animal. I first learned this exercise from Penelope Smith, and it is one of the very best ways to establish an energetic connection with an animal and can be done as often as you like. It can be especially helpful any time you are feeling blocked in understanding an animal friend. Allow plenty of time (at least 15 to 20 minutes) for this exercise. You want to feel unhurried and be able to tune out distractions, so turn off your telephone or retreat to a special place where you know you will not be disturbed; soft lighting and music are also sometimes helpful. Read the exercise thoroughly before beginning.

First, choose an animal you would like to understand better. This can be one of your own animal companions or a wild animal of any species. Sometimes the one you choose may be preempted by another as you enter the meditation. If so, proceed with the one who has appeared unbidden in your uppermost consciousness and trust that there is a reason for you to do this exercise with that animal instead of the one you initially chose.

1. Sit or lie down in a comfortable position. Close your eyes and begin breathing deeply and slowly. Feel yourself sink into the chair or the bed, the floor beneath, and then into the earth. Open your heart and feel love for the animal you are about to work with. While maintaining this deep, slow breathing, mentally scan your body and check for any areas where you may be holding tension. Then, on the inhale, breathe in white light energy, filling any area where you are holding tension, until you feel that tension let go and begin to relax. On the exhale see the tension in that area leave your body with your breath. You may need to repeat this process several times in the same area if it is especially tense. Just keep on until you can feel the tension drain away every time you exhale. Work through your entire body, releasing tension wherever you find it in this same manner. As you go, picture each area relaxing and opening fully.

2. Once you are relaxed and open, do one of the following, whichever best suits your situation:

3. picture your chosen animal in your mind's eye if he is not with you;

4. gaze at a photograph of the animal; or

5. look at the animal himself if he is physically present. Stay quiet and fully present, simply gazing upon the animal and feeling the love in your heart that you hold for him. If you prefer closing your eyes, go ahead and do so and simply focus on a mental picture of the animal. Breathe in a normal but relaxed way and stay aware of any tension in your body or mind that may develop, releasing it on your out-breath.

6. Notice now how the animal breathes—how fast or slow. Compare that to the pace of your own inhalation-exhalation cycle and adjust your breathing to coordinate with that of the animal. Depending upon which animal you are experiencing, this may mean that your breaths perfectly synchronize. Or it may mean that one breath cycle for you is two or more for the animal. Work with it until the two cycles become rhythmically meshed in a harmonious pattern.

7. Very slowly, energetically move yourself around and into the animal's body and point of view. You will now be gazing out at the world through the animal's eyes. Make sure to maintain the synchronized breath pattern between the two of you that you have already established. You are now part of this animal.

8. While staying very relaxed, begin to feel what it's like to be in this animal's body—with paws on the ground, or fins in water, or wings in air. Spend a little time adjusting to the new sensations you are feeling. Everything will be different for you. Then slowly and consciously focus on the animal's physical senses, one at a time, and feel the experience of each: look out through its eyes, taste its favorite food, hear in the way it hears, savor its sense of smell, and experience what it feels like to be touched. Take time

to deeply process what each of these sensations is like. Now shift your focus and become aware of your thoughts and feelings as this animal. How do you feel toward humans or other animals of your own kind or of other kinds? Can you communicate with them, and if so, how do you do that? What is it like when you feel different emotions as this animal: joy, fear, excitement, curiosity, love, anger? Take time with each emotion. Walk yourself through this quiet meditation with the animal and try to experience anything and everything you can imagine that might be in his or her world. Is your vision altered? Many animals have different vision than we do. How do your pulse and breathing rates compare to those of your human self? How is your body temperature and texture different or the same? How do you rest? How do you play? What do you like best about your life? Take some time to enjoy this favorite activity! How do you feel about yourself and your life in general as this animal? Imagine every question you possibly can and fully experience it.

9. Once you have experienced everything you can think of, become aware of your own individual breath once again. Allow it to resume its natural rhythm as separate from the animal's. Then, very, very slowly, move yourself energetically out of the animal and back around to your original position until you are facing it once again. As you gently leave this meditative reverie, thank and honor the animal for letting you experience its essence. You may find yourself feeling lightheaded and dizzy, and perhaps in a state of awe at what you have witnessed and felt.

Practice this exercise often with many different animals. It is not only an amazing experience, but can also serve as an excellent first step in an actual dialogue with a animal.

One of the main things you might notice while doing the above meditation is feeling extreme emotion. You can actually feel an animal's emotions so don't be surprised. It is amazing how many people still seem to think animals do not have emotions but, just like us, they have a wide range. And, just as with humans, each individual animal's emotional experience and makeup is unique to them. Some may be very level-headed, practical, and down-to-earth. They take things in stride and are not easily upset. Others may fluctuate wildly in their emotionality—excited one minute, doubtful or fearful the next; curious about one thing but then easily distracted by something else. Be ready for anything and don't have any preconceptions in this area.

(NOTE: Since this meditation involves projecting oneself into an animal's interior space psychically, the question of "permission" arises. If the animal is one of your own animal companions, there is rarely a problem with your exploring their inner territory. Likewise, should an animal force itself into your consciousness in this exercise, permission for you to experience its essence is a given. If you have any reservations about whether you are welcome psychically for the purposes of this exercise, simply ask if it's okay. You'll know if it's not, OR you won't be allowed "in." If, for any reason, you feel it is not right to proceed with this exercise with any particular animal, retreat and choose another.)

CHAPTER EIGHT

HOW INFORMATION IS SENT AND RECEIVED

As you begin to transmit and receive impressions and messages, they may take many forms. Every animal communicator has his or her most effective techniques for sending and receiving information, but it takes a while to learn and refine your own style. Remember, be ready for anything! Everyone has different strengths and weaknesses in this area, so don't compare your own experience to anyone else's.

IG

One of the most common ways of sending and receiving information telepathically is through pictures. Animals readily see pictures we are holding in our mind, especially if those pictures relate to them. For this reason, when using pictures to convey a thought or idea, always see a picture of what you *want* from the animal, not what you *don't want*. For example, if you are communicating with a Rottweiler about why he should stop jumping up on people to greet them, you do not want to visualize him doing that while you're talking to him. Instead, you want to see and show him a picture of himself sitting or standing quietly with all four feet on the ground.

Animals seem to have a great knack for showing pictures to us too. When talking to an animal telepathically and awaiting a response, you may suddenly "see" a picture mentally. Don't question it. This is a message, or part of a message, the animal is sending back to you. If you don't understand what it means you can ask the animal to please elaborate a bit more. Or just wait—the meaning may become clear as you get further into the conversation.

HEARING

Often a picture will be accompanied by words or ideas that you more or less "hear" in your mind. Or you may hear these words and ideas *without* a picture. Sometimes you might even "hear" a specific voice quality. If you are communicating with an animal at the owner's request, it is useful to make note of the exact words you get, as certain words may mean something very special to that person, even though they make no sense to you at all. Usually these ideas or words, especially when combined with the pictures, will be all the information you need to understand the message. You can also use words to convey an idea to the animal. Often, however, the animal will benefit by attendant mental pictures or feelings that amplify the meaning of words.

Again, you may ask for clarification if you need it, but don't keep asking the same question over and over just to make sure you're getting it right. This will take you into a place of mental doubt and over-thinking rather than openness, and your receptivity will be compromised or may shut down completely.

TOUCH AND SMELL

Less common than pictures or words are the modes of sending and receiving information through the senses of touch and smell. Some people do experience these literally, so stay open to them. As with seeing and hearing, you may feel and smell, but not always in a literal or physical way. That said, if you are working with an animal remotely and want to pet or stroke it, both the animal and you will experience that "touch" sensation on some level. So feel free to hold, pet, and stroke whenever it feels right.

KNOWINGNESS

Sometimes when you are communicating and you have asked a question or inquired into a situation, you will all of a sudden just know everything at once about the answer. This knowing might include entire scenarios from the animal's past, understanding how they feel about it now, and questions they might have about the future. Likewise, while conveying a thought or picture to the animal, you may suddenly realize that he or she immediately knows the entire idea you are trying to convey, even before you're finished.

These broad gestalt impressions can be so all-encompassing that you hardly know where to begin as you start trying to describe or translate them. One might say that this is the most complete way of sending and receiving information, and most people experience it at one time or another. Instead of getting one sentence at a time, you get the whole chapter... or even the whole book!

The first time you receive this kind of global message from an animal, you will have a different awareness of what interspecies communication can be, and you will probably have stepped into a higher level of telepathic skill. And yet, for some of you this may happen right away, just as soon as you put your mind and intention to communicating with animals. In fact, some people may never get words or pictures, but may always receive information by just knowing.

EMOTIONS AND FEELINGS

Sending and receiving emotions and feelings is another common way information is conveyed between a person and an animal, and perhaps one of the most effective. As you will learn through the energy projection exercises later in this chapter, it is easier to project a message if there is strong emotion attached. This is a skill you can develop to enhance the effectiveness of telepathic messages you project to an animal. Receiving information back from them in the form of emotions, and actually experiencing those emotions, is what is called "empathic" understanding and, while extremely valuable, can also be one of the most difficult abilities to handle while you're learning to communicate.

Here's why! If you are suddenly hit with a very strong emotion, it can literally cripple your energy flow and terminate your communication until you clear it out of your body and psyche. Many of us, especially if we're psychic to any degree, are also empathic, so we pick up the feelings and thoughts of those around us. We often don't realize this is happening and so may confuse those thoughts and feelings with our own. We may find ourselves feeling very drained or sad after going to the grocery store, for example, because we empathically picked up someone else's grief.

IF YOU ARE AN EMPATH…

It is very important, as you refine your communication skills, to be able to determine which feelings are yours as opposed to any that might be coming from outside yourself. This way you can remain clear for accurate reception. If an animal allows you to feel what they are feeling, you may experience pain or discomfort, either physically or emotionally. Ask them if this is what they are feeling, and if it is, thank them for sharing it with you. Let them know you feel it and how much you sympathize with them. Tell them the information is helpful, and then either allow them to take the feeling back or, with their permission and if you know how, help transmute this energy for a higher purpose by either grounding it out or offering it up to the light.

Empaths have the hardest time when learning to communicate with animals because they are literally sponges for emotional sensations and impressions. They may be flooded by these in a way they do not understand as they open themselves up to become more receptive. If this is one of your strong areas, you might consider studying psychic protection and clearing so that you can recognize emotional or physical sensations that are not your own and can learn how to re-stabilize yourself after experiencing them. The following story underlines just how important this can be.

THE SAD CASE OF ONE VERY EMPATHIC ANIMAL COMMUNICATION STUDENT

This is an example of how deeply empathic perception can impact one's life, and how important it can be to get a handle on that particular aspect of consciousness.

Many years ago, I had a lovely, gentle-spirited lady in one of my animal communication classes, whom I will call Marge. As with every student, Marge adored animals and so her impetus for attending class was to understand them better. This was a three-day class where we went from beginner-level to intermediate. We had many animals as subjects, both live and in photographs.

As is usual in such classes, we progressed through increasingly complex levels of communication, doing exercises in which everyone engaged in silent conversations with animals and took notes on what they received. At the end of each exercise each member of the class shared his or her experience with the rest of the class, reading from their notes and giving his or her impressions of their conversation.

I couldn't help but notice that every time Marge shared a conversation she had just had with an animal, she was in tears and only reported on the sad or difficult aspects of life the animal she had just talked with might have experienced, whether past or present. After a few such reports, it was obvious to me that Marge had a proclivity for identifying with this type of information empathically, so this was the perfect lead-in for me to talk about this particular way of receiving, and how important it is to learn how to work with it so as not to allow it to affect us too strongly. I thought everyone understood. But throughout the class, all Marge continued to pick up from her subjects were the hard times they had experienced. Marge was virtually in tears all weekend.

A couple of months later another member of the class called me unexpectedly and told me Marge had committed suicide. Of course I was shocked, and I don't remember that conversation very well, but I do remember thinking at the time that someone with Marge's incredible empathic ability, which unfortunately identified mostly with grief and sadness, would not be a surprising candidate for suicide.

EXERCISES AND MEDITATIONS FOR THE EMPATH

The following exercises and meditations are offered to help you stay clear and protect yourself from uninvited influences, as well as to strengthen yourself from within. I love this first exercise because it is proactive rather than defensive, and focuses on building internal power within rather than building an outside wall.

STRENGTHENING YOUR INTERNAL ENERGY

1. Find a quiet space without distractions, relax and begin breathing deeply and slowly. Visualize the center of your physical body as a vibrant, luminous core with the power to generate and distribute mental, physical, and spiritual growth energy. See this core as a glowing ball of fire in your solar plexus—just above and behind your naval. Focus on this glowing ball of energy until you can see it clearly and feel it strongly.

2. While continuing to visualize, place the fingertips of both hands over this glowing core at your solar plexus and begin expanding and flowing its revitalizing energy throughout your body. You may feel tingling in your fingertips, hands, or even up your arms. Use your intention and your will to create this expansion, and see and feel the energy filling every fiber of your being. Take as much time as you need during this part of the exercise.

3. Continue to focus and visualize and, if you like, expand the energy until it surrounds the outside of your physical body. Eventually you will be able to project this energy as far out as you like.

4. While holding the energy, repeat the following mantra or any other mantra you create that feels reassuring and protective to you: *"I am now empowered and secure in mind, body, and spirit."* Repeat the mantra several times, noticing how strong you feel.

Use Step 2 and repeat your mantra, out loud or silently, any time you feel the need to protect yourself or build your own inner strength. The more you use this cue, the faster it will work to protect and empower you.

TWO BIG WARRIORS

If you have not quite perfected the above exercise, or still need a quiet, meditative space when employing it and don't have much time, try this. Picture two big Indian chiefs in full headdress and war paint, ten feet tall, one standing behind each of your shoulders. These are intimidating guys to everyone else, but they are your friends and are here to protect you. You can even name them if you like.

Take your chiefs with you into any daunting or scary situation—even into a difficult meeting with your boss—or ask them to stand with you any time you fear someone else's energy may overtake your own. Knowing that they've got your back will help you feel protected and project more self-confidence and energy from within your core being. And, of course, thank your chiefs for helping you out.

THE BLUE RIBBON EXERCISE – CLEARING GRIEF

Here is a helpful exercise to help you clear, on the spot, any emotion that is interfering with or blocking your communication, whether it is one you have picked up empathically or one you are experiencing subjectively. Practice this exercise until you are very comfortable with it, because when you need it suddenly you will want to be able to do it quickly (in the middle of an animal communication session, for instance). We will use the emotion of grief for this example.

Take a moment to close your eyes, breathe deeply, and center yourself.

1. Picture your heart chakra with "heart doors" in the front of your chest that can be opened or closed, at your discretion. These doors can be any style or any color you choose. Whatever you envision is what will work for you. Open your heart doors.

2. Picture and feel your crown chakra opening widely.

3. Picture a beautiful wide blue ribbon coming down from the Heavens, into your crown chakra, and down into your heart chakra, where it then flows out your heart doors and into infinity. This ribbon is moving continuously, flowing from Heaven, through you, and then into infinity. See it as a river that is ever present and ever-flowing. (If the ribbon in your mind's eye is red or yellow or pink, that's okay too. Whatever you "see" that feels right for you will work.)

4. Now picture the emotion you would like to divest yourself of—in this example, grief—and place it on the ribbon, inside your chest. Picture it in any form you like.

5. On your out-breath, see the emotion ride out of your heart doors on the blue ribbon and watch it as it moves on into infinity. *Feel* the change as this emotion leaves your being and the clarity you experience as you resume whatever activity it was blocking. You can place the emotion on the ribbon and watch it ride away as many times as you like until you feel this change. And don't

worry… you'll know when the emotion has left your being—you'll feel clear as a bell!

BUILD ON YOUR STRENGTHS

It is very important to take note of how you most easily send and receive information when you first begin animal communication. Most people initially receive in one or two ways only. Once you are able to identify your own best techniques, work on those and fine tune them. The more you use them, the faster they will come and the more effective they will be. At some point you will notice that you are sending and receiving in other ways as well. Modes of communication may vary with each animal also, as animals themselves have their own unique ability and style of communicating, so with each animal you may find yourself going through an initial process of finding the right "language" in terms of how you can best talk to each other. One animal may never give you anything but vague mental impressions, the next might chatter up a storm and show you pictures the entire time he is talking to you. Matching your styles will be fairly automatic the more adept you become at telepathic communication. Again, be receptive and open to whatever comes and to the essence of each animal you encounter.

CHAPTER NINE

LEARNING TO SEND & RECEIVE INFORMATION
TELEPATHICALLY

Earlier in the book we talked about how we constantly exchange energetic vibrations with each other, our animal companions, and the world in general (remember the example about talking to a person on the phone and knowing he's angry even when you can't see his face and he keeps an even tone of voice?). Communicating with animals is no different—you just have to learn how to channel and use the skills of projecting and sensing energy in a deliberate and specific way. Along with that, keeping your heart open and your emotions engaged are your two best tools for communicating with animals.

"I wear my heart on my sleeve" is your best motto now!

EXERCISES FOR PROJECTING ENERGY

One very simple and effective way to learn to project and then retract, or pull back, your own energy at will, and then, later, use that ability to send and receive telepathic information, is to practice *Rolling the Beach Ball*, below.

ROLLING THE BEACH BALL

1. Get together with a human partner if you can and sit on the floor facing each other about ten feet apart. If you don't have a human partner handy, visualize someone you really like sitting across from you. Close your eyes, take a few deep breaths, and relax.

2. Imagine that you have a big red beach ball sitting on the floor in front of you and look at the ball in your mind's eye. (If your ball is blue, or yellow, or purple, or any other color, that's fine, but red usually works well, as it is an "action" color.) Gently push the ball so it rolls over to your partner while watching and feeling your point of focus (the ball) moving with it. Next, see your friend push the ball and watch it roll it back to you, again feeling your point of focus change as the ball approaches. In this way, roll the ball back and forth a few times. Take as much time as you need. You should be able to actually feel your visual focus change as it follows the ball out and then back, even with your eyes closed.

3. Now put a strong emotion inside the beach ball ("I love you" usually works well) and roll it to your partner. Don't worry about *how* to do this, just do it! The stronger you can feel the emotion you are sending in the ball, the better! Again, visually follow the ball as it rolls away from you and at the same time also *feel* that part of you that generates the emotion you are sending as it leaves your immediate energy field. Really focus on the message and the feeling behind it, and you will be better able to feel its energy as it moves away. In fact, that energy isn't really *leaving* you at all—rather, it is a part of you that is expanding outward toward your partner.

4. Watch the ball and feel the emotion until it touches your partner. When this occurs, you are psychically in your partner's space with your energy body, and you should be able to actually feel or sense when that contact is made.

5. Again have your partner push the ball back to you, visually watch it approach, and notice what it feels like as the emotion you put into the ball returns to you and leaves your partner's psychic space. This is your own emotion coming back to you. Your energy field is expanding when you roll the ball to your partner and contracting when it rolls back to you. The process may feel almost like inhaling and exhaling.

6. Take your time, rolling the ball slowly back and forth so that you can really experience what it's like to *send* part of yourself out to touch a remote target with your energy, and then *feel* when you've pulled it back into yourself. Again, if you don't have an actual partner, just imagine someone you care for opposite you who can push that ball back to you each time you request it.

The more you do this exercise, the easier it will become, and the more readily you will be able to feel your energy coming and going under your own direction. Learning to pull your energy back in and feel its return to you is as important as learning to project it.

ROLLING THE BEACH BALL WITH YOUR ANIMAL COMPANION

Once you feel comfortable with this exercise, go ahead and try an initial simple communication with an animal companion using the same process. If you are able to make contact and get a response, the energy you feel returning to you will feel different. It will not be your own, but rather that of the animal as it enters your own psychic space.

Using the same steps as above, put your animal companion's name and a simple greeting like "Hi, how are you?" into your big red beach ball and roll it toward them. If you are able to project this energy and message effectively, they will either send the ball back to you, or perhaps just a quick response. Usually their responses are faster than your beach ball. Be prepared to hear your animal's reply in your head, possibly with a unique voice quality, or possibly to have a picture pop into your consciousness. Even if you hear the reply in your own voice, the style of speech and the "feel" will be a lot different than if you had initiated it yourself. Once you have connected with them in this way, you can keep the communication going by rolling the beach ball back again with other simple messages.

This exercise will give you an idea of what it's like to actually register energetic contact from another source. You will also begin finding out in what form you are best able to receive information telepathically at this point. Did you see pictures, hear words, feel a touch? And remember, the more emotion you feel when you project a message, the stronger it will be conveyed—even if the emotion is curiosity or just a sense of fun! And soon you won't need the beach ball at all!

The Water Balloon "Hello" – Getting Their Attention!

Once you start conversing with animals, if you feel you're having trouble getting their attention, try this.

1. Visualize holding a cartoon bubble or water balloon and put the animal's name inside it.

2. While mentally calling the animal's name, gently "toss" the bubble or balloon so that it lands softly on the animal's shoulders.

3. If you don't get the animal's attention with the first balloon, try a couple more. They will usually hear you at least by the third balloon. (Please note: Some animals do not appreciate this action, in which case an apology and explanation may be in order! Most, however, don't mind it at all, and may not even seem to notice the "water balloon" landing on their shoulders... but they *will* hear you calling them.)

4. Once you have an animal's attention, introduce yourself and ask if they would be willing to talk to you.

5. No matter what, whether you have an actual conversation or not, when you sign off or say goodbye to the animal, thank him or her profusely for allowing you to tune in!

CHAPTER TEN

RELEASING DOUBT AND DEVELOPING PATIENCE

So far you've learned to switch between Beta and Alpha brainwaves, send thoughts and emotions to a target and bring them back, and send and receive simple messages to and from your animal companion. Somewhere along the way, you've probably begun to doubt the process or your ability. By now you might be wondering whether any of this is "real" or whether you've really gotten anything back from your animal friends... or something else, like: "Am I just making this up in my head?"

Don't worry! Doubt is a natural part of the process, and it is the single biggest hurdle in learning to exercise your telepathic muscles. In animal communication classes students usually move through the preparatory exercises and discussion without a lot of difficulty. They begin to feel relaxed and safe, surrounded by a group of like-minded souls who are all laughing, sharing, and excited about the process.

But when it comes time to talk to an animal for the first time in class (gulp!), they suddenly become very nervous and self-doubting. There goes their nice relaxed state and those Alpha brainwaves we've been working on activating.

THE DOUBT BOX

Okay, time out.

Here we will digress and talk about how self-doubt is everyone's— EVERYONE'S—biggest nemesis, and what we can do about it. Everyone thinks, "Oh yikes! I'll never be able to do this!" Relax. You'll do fine. When you find yourself feeling skeptical or nervous, use the technique I teach in my classes: Build a doubt box!

BUILDING YOUR DOUBT BOX

In class we all build doubt boxes together, and then we good-naturedly remind each other throughout the workshop to make good use of them. But you don't need a class for this to work for you. Here's how to build your doubt box and how to use it.

1. Build a box out of energy using your hands. Visualize the box and, using your hands as if you were handling an actual physical box, first "hold" the top and bottom, then the ends, then the front and back, and tap or "glue" them together manually. You can use any materials and colors you like, and your box can be any size you

like. Leave a slot or opening in the top of the box. Don't worry about how to do this; your hands and your intention will naturally project the energy needed to build this box. Build the box in the air right in front of you, until you can see, feel, and sense the presence of your box. You can make your box as large or small as you like. This exercise is so pre-occupying and "visual," that in and of itself it will help you relax. Knowing that others have the same fears and concerns you do helps a lot too. In a class setting, this small "community project" has the effect of bringing everyone's anxieties out into the open and allows them to begin dissipating. But if you're doing it by yourself, don't feel silly... just trust that your doubt box is going to be your best friend in overcoming one of the main hurdles you will encounter when starting to talk to animals.

2. Set the box down beside you or make sure it is nearby and handy any time you are talking to an animal. Any time you feel doubt, panic or other negative emotions creeping in, reach up with your hand (literally) and just pluck it out of your head with your fingers and put it in your box. In a class setting we gently remind each other to "put it in the box" any time one of us starts expressing self-doubt. Soon, everyone is laughing as they find themselves frequently reaching up to pluck "doubt" out of their head and drop it in their box!

3. If you feel your box getting full, just push it down into the earth and start a new box. Build and dump boxes as often as you like, until you don't need them any more.

Once doubt has been addressed openly and dealt with head on, you'll find yourself more readily noticing when it kicks in and more easily being able to put it in your box so that it doesn't get in the way of your progress. By redirecting your thoughts in this manner, you are literally retraining your brain to use other neural pathways and processes than those it is used to using. Part of you is telling another part of you that you honor and acknowledge any feelings and thoughts that may come up, and that you will make a legitimate space for them, but that you will not allow them to override your intent. Once you have used your doubt box for a while, and have begun reshaping your thought patterns, you will find that doubts are popping into your mind much less frequently and that you are needing your doubt box less and less. Eventually you will forget about your doubt box altogether.

PATIENCE, PATIENCE!

Even without doubts to hold you back, you may experience yet other obstacles that are difficult to master in your efforts to learn animal communication. For instance, when you begin simple communications with an animal, you may be inclined at first to think you are getting nothing if you don't get an immediate response after sending a message. Not necessarily so! Remember, this is unfamiliar territory. Animals certainly can send back a response instantaneously, as noted in the beach ball exercise, but sometimes they don't. They may need time to think about their answer. OR their answer may come in a form you are not yet able to recognize or didn't expect. Give yourself a break! Put your doubt in your doubt box and remind yourself to relax. Do a body scan. Take a few deep breaths, slow down, and quiet your "mind-chatter." Don't clench (check your jaw). Don't over-try. Stay humble and open, be patient, and *just wait.*

Visualize or look at the animal with the sole intention of somehow experiencing whatever the animal wants you to experience or may choose to share with you. Give it several minutes. If you notice doubts still coming in, good! Noticing them is all important in learning to handle them. Don't give yourself a hard time for having them, but instead just acknowledge them and pluck them away, dropping them into your doubt box. Close your eyes if it helps. Slow your breathing. You can resend your thought or question if you like, then be still. Be Buddha. I can almost guarantee that you will receive something back from the animal. It may only be an impression. It may even be an impression that lets you know he or she does not want to communicate or is trying to "hide." Fine. Then that in and of itself is the response. Honor and accept what you get and do not question it. Do not ask the animal the same question over and over in order to "double check" what you are getting. Accept it, thank the animal, and move on. (Note: Remember also, when you feel blocked in a communication, if you have the time, you can always do the meditation for getting into the animal's point of view. This will most assuredly enhance your receptivity and ease the communication process.)

LETTING GO OF OPINIONS AND STAYING OPEN

Now that you've got some ways to handle your doubt and muster your patience, you need to think again about one more thing—your own attitudes, opinions, and judgments. In Chapter Five we talked about why this is important ethically and theoretically, but now let's look at how opinion or judgment can actually be an impediment to receiving information from an animal accurately.

Look at it this way: the more relaxed and open you remain while practicing animal communication (the Alpha state), the better you can receive information. If you are holding judgments and opinions about what's going to happen (or what you *want* to happen), you will be tense and tight and your energy will contract and your receptivity will close down. You will be operating in a left-brained, Beta brainwave state. Remember how open-mindedness goes hand-in-hand with the Alpha state? *This* is what you want! Going into a communication with strong opinions or attitudes (i.e. being in a "Beta" frame of mind) could be compared to a sighted person who is determined to read Braille numbers in an elevator in order to find his floor. Your opinions and attitudes can dictate so strongly what and how you perceive things that anything that doesn't fit within those left-brained parameters will not be recognized at all.

Now is the time to table all your thoughts, attitudes, and opinions about what "horse" or "dog" or "snake" means to you personally—or for that matter, in your culture, in medicine, or in any other context you might have been exposed to. Honor that all beings have their own innate essence that is unique to them and very different from yours. Likewise, each species has genetic predilections that shape its behaviors, thought patterns, and survival skills. Realize that you are basically entering this territory fairly ignorant of what really motivates various animal species. Allow this to humble you and help open you for the magical and astonishing revelations that can then come to you through these wonderful beings. Being in a relaxed, open state of mind unclouded by opinions and judgments is essential for this process. It is fine to put opinions and judgments in your doubt box too, by the way. Don't beat yourself up about them; just notice them, don't be attached to them, and move on. Your opinions are very likely to be changed radically anyway, once you've spoken with a few members of the animal kingdom.

THE STARTLING CASE OF "GYPSY" – BE READY FOR ANYTHING!

As you begin animal communication, a key point to keep in mind, *always*, is:

BE READY FOR ANYTHING! There are surprises in store!

Here is an account of what happened in one of my basic animal communication classes that illustrates this point very well. As this case demonstrates, it's important that you be prepared for the unexpected and bizarre.

Class was being hosted by one of my clients and her animal companion, a recently rescued female dog named Gypsy. It was the second day of class, and participants had brought their animals so that we might begin the actual communication process with them. We were starting our very first such exercise which is the simplest imaginable greeting (in fact, at this point I encourage students to use their imagination and "play like" they get something back from the animal if they need to). We had ten students and several dogs and cats in the room. Gypsy was in the same spot where she had been all weekend, parked in a doorway between the group and the rest of her house. The students paired off, each pair choosing one dog or cat to speak to. The partners then took turns doing the exercise: they each, separately, sent a simple greeting to the dog or cat, such as, "Hello, how are you?" and then waited openly to see what they would get back. They did not tell each other what they got back from the animal.

At this stage the doubt boxes were being heavily used and everyone was nervous, so I reminded them to imagine receiving a reply (having the leeway to use your imagination at this stage seems to take off some of the pressure for most students—you can try this yourself when you are in doubt—besides using your doubt box, of course). We took plenty of time for this first exercise. When everyone was finished, we went around the room and each person shared what greeting they had extended to their designated animal and what acknowledgement they had received back. The results were typical. Almost everyone got an acknowledgement of some sort—a word, a look, an idea. One or two perhaps thought they didn't get anything but had a sense their animal had definitely heard them. None thought that what they had experienced was "just their imagination."

We got to the last pair, a woman and a man who had never met before class. These two had greeted Gypsy. The woman was hesitant and flustered and blushing when she reported to us that, after she said "Hello" to Gypsy, Gypsy quickly flipped back to her, "F____ off!" The poor woman was so embarrassed and so confused by this that she was half laughing and half in tears. Before she could even finish quoting Gypsy, her partner dropped his notebook and his jaw and said, "That's what she yelled at me too! Only for me it was "Get the f____ off my property!" The class started laughing uproariously. Obviously this was the best confirmation those two could possibly have had that they had actually made contact with this dog, but they were both so flabbergasted by what she had said that it left them speechless. This is the best possible example of the rule: "Be ready for anything!" (As for Gypsy, we continued to work with her throughout the day and later as well. We learned that she had come from a very chaotic and violent former home where there was lots of shouting and cursing, and she had lots of issues about her territory and abandonment. Within a few weeks, and with love and understanding, Gypsy was doing great, loved her new home, and was fiercely loyal to her adopted family.)

As in the case of Gypsy, it is good to know that, unless an animal has shut down totally emotionally or has some physiological anomaly, all of them respond to love on some level. Love and understanding can soften and begin the healing of a multitude of emotional wounds and other problems. If you can leave a problem-solving communication session with even just enough understanding to have made the first chink in the emotional armor of a defensive or shut-down animal, you have begun a very important process. Let them know you understand and empathize with what they have experienced (this may be something that happened to them or perhaps just how they are feeling). Tell them that you and their person are very sorry, that it will never happen again (if you know this to be true), and that you fully honor what they have been through (or are experiencing now). Thank them for sharing their experience with you; their having done so is a great honor. Even this small acknowledgement of their pain can begin their healing. If you have felt their feelings empathically, this will not be hard to do sincerely. The depth of pain—and joy—animals are capable of feeling is astounding.

CHAPTER ELEVEN

MOVING FORWARD

Now that you have been initiated, have your doubts all neatly arranged in a box, and have had it verified that you are actually communicating successfully with animals, you can dive into all kinds of topics with the animals you talk to. Here are some sample questions you might begin to play with as you practice.

QUESTIONS FOR GETTING TO KNOW YOU

❖ What do you like about being a (dog/cat,etc.)?

❖ How do you feel about the shape, size, color of your body?

❖ What do you like the most about your life?

❖ What do you like the least about your life?

❖ How do you feel about your environment?

❖ What would you like to change about your life?

❖ How do you feel about humans?

❖ How is your health? Do you have any pain? If so, where?

❖ What is your purpose in life?

❖ Tell me about your family (animals, persons).

❖ Tell me about your dreams.

❖ How do you feel about other members of your species? Other species?

❖ What can you do as (a dog/cat, etc.) that makes you feel proud?

❖ How can I better understand you?

❖ Do you have a job? What is it?

❖ How do you have fun?

❖ What would you like to ask/tell me?

❖ What would you like to know about me?

Have fun! Be patient! And put your fears and hesitations in that doubt box!!

Chapter Twelve

Talking to The Wild Kingdom

Many people are interested in talking to wild animals, and in communicating with plants as well, and I am often asked if the process is the same as with our domesticated species. The answer, at least for most of us, is, "Not usually." Because animals in the wild are operating much more strongly according to their instincts and their species' particular survival needs, they are less inclined to tune into us individually than their domesticated counterparts. There are certainly exceptions, and much wisdom can be learned from an individual animal in the wild, but often establishing contact is through different methods than those described in this book and may involve invoking other outside entities and energies to help us connect with them.

The Devic realm, in particular, is a powerful ally in this pursuit. Devas are forms of invisible intelligence that hold the "blueprints" and knowledge about everything in the natural world and yet are specific to their specialty, their particular species or sub-species, or even for their specific herd or garden. They sort of "know everything," if you will, and are often quite willing to help us "hold hands" with their physical counterparts in order to have a communion. Working on this level is, for most of us, a step beyond communicating with our domesticated friends. It is not harder than the former, but requires an ability to invoke help from and talk directly to the intermediaries (Devas) that rule nature. For some this involves a greater leap of faith than just talking to their dog does, so, admittedly, the idea may take some getting used to.

Talking to wild animals and plants is spell-binding and will usher you into yet another new level of experience. It can be awesome and overwhelming as you begin to enter these worlds beyond the familiar, and the wisdom held and imparted is spectacular and eye-opening.

There are rare individuals, of course, who are so open and naturally connected to the great Oneness that other beings of all kinds, including wild animals, flock to them. St. Francis of Assisi was one such individual, and you should consider yourself blessed if you have this natural proclivity. Even St. Francis, however, went through a spiritual growth process before he achieved this state. Hopefully, as we continue to close the gaps in understanding among the beings on our planet and beyond, there will be more and more of us who fall into this category.

Chapter Thirteen

The Case of Jack, the Stubborn Mule

A Verbatim Example of an Animal Communication Session

The following is an actual case which, on its face, was fairly simple but which ended up being multi-faceted and complex. It contains examples of many things the animal communicator must keep in mind when working her way through a situation that involves problem solving. This particular case was conducted by phone, and a verbatim transcript is set out below. Actual words spoken by the animal (**J**) or myself (**L**) are in italics; information I received or transmitted through other modes (thoughts, pictures, etc.) is in parentheses.

Mandy, the client, was the proud owner of a four-year-old male mule gelding named Jack whom she purchased as a yearling. Mandy was a holistic equine veterinarian schooled in many alternative modalities and had a thriving practice in a major U.S. city. She was a leader in alternative vet care for many years and was brilliant and open-minded in her work. She regularly had cases referred to her that even the finest veterinary schools had written off and usually sent them home well and thriving. Mandy had been a mule devotee for a long time, so she also had a 20+-yr.-old mare mule named Bess. She and Bess had "grown up" together in terms of learning about stubbornness and how to deal with each other. (There is a good reason the mule is portrayed as the epitome of stubbornness!) After 20 years of trying to "train" Bess the hard way, Mandy had finally become a dedicated student of natural horsemanship. Force and obstinacy, which go hand-in-hand with the old training methods, are a mule's native language, so to speak, so a person can never win using those techniques. Plug in the newer training approaches involving patience but firmness, consistency with variety, and gentle reward, and voila—a new way that works, even with mules! Mules mature slowly however, so Mandy had her hands full—natural horsemanship or no natural horsemanship—with Jack.

Mandy called requesting an appointment because Jack had bucked her off during one of their training sessions. This was the first time this had happened. Mandy wanted to understand Jack's version of this incident and to make sure Jack didn't now think he could get her off his back any time he wanted.

INSIGHTS: *This was a loaded situation in several respects. There was fear and the possibility of bodily injury involved so it was a case to be taken very seriously. I had known and worked with Mandy for many years with all her animals and had known and worked with Jack since she got him.*

Mandy was also a personal friend so I knew her personality and foibles. I also knew her history with Jack as well as everything he had told or conveyed to us before this particular session. I was automatically "set up" each time I worked with Mandy to possibly be influenced by what I already knew.

The important question to myself then, as a responsible animal communicator, was, "Am I clear enough to conduct this communication effectively and without letting my subjective view of the situation interfere with what I receive about it?" Since Mandy was a friend, the answer to this question might easily have been "no" because I might have been too emotionally involved in her current circumstance to be objective. At the time, however, I felt very clear and like I could receive and convey information objectively and effectively.

Mandy was a good client. She understood the importance of maintaining a professional demeanor when we were working together in this way, and she was able to do that very well. Sometimes close friends or clients are not able to do that. Only you can evaluate the climate of your personal relationship with a client or friend and make the decision as to whether you can be professional and effective in any given animal communication case.

BACKGROUND AS MANDY GAVE IT TO ME AT THE TIME OF OUR APPOINTMENT:

Tuesday of the previous week Jack had gone in his horse trailer with Mandy on her veterinary horse calls. Prior to that, she had taken him on calls occasionally just for the exposure to new situations, loading and unloading in the trailer, and experiencing longer hauls. During these "practice" days, Jack was sometimes taken out of the trailer, sometimes tied to the trailer, and sometimes he stayed in the trailer. On occasion Mandy would ride him briefly somewhere along the way, but often she did not.

This particular day was a very long one—about 12 hours. The previous Saturday Mandy had taken Jack to a rodeo and let him "hang out," again just for exposure and practice.

On Wednesday, mid-day, when Mandy went out to ride Jack, he was easy to catch but began acting nervous and tentative when they came in to tack up and he had to walk near the trailer. He was trying to "sit back" (pull back on his lead rope) and didn't want to go anywhere near that trailer! Once she got on him he still would not go near it and was very fidgety and spooky. Therefore, instead of taking him out for a trail ride, Mandy worked with Jack for an hour and a half or so around the trailer, doing exercises and other activities. She finally got him into a relaxed state where she could ride him back and forth and could go up and touch the trailer. At the end of the session, she began practicing some steering with her legs. At this point, Jack's "relaxed state" had lulled him to the point where he had literally "zoned out" and quit paying attention, so Mandy touched him gently with her spur (which she had done often before). Jack literally exploded, and Mandy went flying off and landed in the brush. Jack became immediately quiet again, swung around and looked at her with a puzzled expression on his face, as if to say, "What are you doing down there?" He didn't seem agitated at all.

Mandy then pointed out that she had a fairly new batch of hay that she had noticed seemed to make several of the horses in the barn very nervous and "wired." Jack had been eating this hay at the time of the bucking incident. Also, the wind was up that day and there were gunshots being fired on property nearby.

QUESTIONS AND POINTS MANDY WANTED COVERED IN OUR

SESSION:

- ❖ What did Jack think of the trailering days where he went with her on calls?

- ❖ Why was he so nervous that Wednesday around the trailer?

- ❖ What had gone on in his mind when he bucked her off, and why did he do it?

- ❖ Did the new hay have anything to do with his reaction that day?

- ❖ She also wanted me to let Jack know in no uncertain terms that bucking her off was not an option—ever!

INSIGHTS: *It is always important to get the client's idea of what has occurred or what the problem is. I usually ask them to "Tell me why you're calling" (or emailing) because I can then get a description from them in their own words rather than just answers to leading questions I might ask. Then I ask them to tell me what they want to know (what they want me to find out from the animal) and what they want me to tell the animal on their behalf.*

In this case. Mandy gave me five questions or points to cover. Usually three to five questions or topics is plenty for a regular session, and working through them will take between 30 minutes to one hour, depending upon how the communicator works. This session took about an hour.

THE SESSION ITSELF:

Finding and tuning into Jack was easy since I had talked to him many times. There was, therefore, no need for an extensive introduction. In this session, as I tuned into him, I instantly got three impressions, pretty much all at once:

❖ Jack was not present mentally AT ALL at the moment of bucking Mandy off.

❖ He was feeling overwhelmed from a combination of the recent trailering episodes and then an hour and a half of work that day. He had finally just "checked out," so was in la-la land when he felt Mandy's spur. It shocked him!

❖ He had some definite concerns about all this trailering, so he was feeling insecure. He was confused about it. Why were they doing it? Why were they visiting these particular places? Was he supposed to do something there? Was he going to be left at one of them? Again, it totally overwhelmed him.

INSIGHTS: This initial tuning-in period can be very telling and insightful. Trust what you get and use it as a base to build your communication around. You may see pictures of the animal doing certain things or looking a certain way—symbolic body language—that will mean something. You may experience feelings the animal is feeling, emotional or physical. You may sense the general overall "tone" of the animal at the moment (nervous, scared, peaceful, curious, etc.). Make notes on what you get and feel when you first tune into the animal. In this case I got a lot of information that conveyed Jack's concern and confusion during this initial tune-in period. Sometimes you will not get such a complete picture... OR you may not get anything at all. You may just get feelings, thoughts, or images that don't make any sense. Take what you get and use it to help you flesh out all the nuances surrounding the subject of the communication session. Do not, however, use it to "lead" the animal. Let him speak for himself and then see how his thoughts and comments mesh with your initial impressions.

L: *Jack?* (As I call his name, Jack whips his head up. He thinks Mandy is mad at him. He wonders where she is and what's going to happen.)

J: *What do you want?* (He wonders what they are going to do next? He shows me blurry pictures that are a combination of their work and the trailering around all over the place—he shows me he gets motion sick often, and as he shows me this I instantly feel nausea. It makes him miserable.)

L: *Thank you for showing us that! That makes perfect sense. We would like to explain to you what this trailering is all about.* (Then I told and showed him it's just for exposure, practice, etc.). *You are not going to be left somewhere! Don't worry!*

J: (He shows me he often wonders if they are going to a training clinic. He is often confused because he never knows what to expect.)

L: *Well, that's part of the reason for doing it, but only part. In your lifetime you will go many, many places with Mandy and you will be doing lots of different things and going for different reasons. And it is all meant to be enjoyable.*

J: (He goes right back to the issue of motion sickness. That's really a problem for him, and he's very preoccupied with it when we are discussing moving about in the trailer, no matter what the context. How can anything be enjoyable if he's feeling sick!)

INSIGHTS: At this point, I put Jack on hold and tell him I need to talk to Mandy and let her know about this. It just so happens, the information he has given us about motion sickness jibes closely with a pattern of digestive upset he gets into when he is nervous or stressed, as at a training clinic or in new situations sometimes. Mandy and I have a rather extensive discussion of what remedies and aids she can use to handle Jack's motion sickness and come up with a good plan. I chose to have this discussion with her at this point in the communication so I could then tell Jack what to expect in the future about this problem. If action is to be taken, it is important to let the animal know what to expect. Notice, we have not begun to address the key issue—the bucking—but Jack is way too preoccupied with his discomfort and confusion to move on to any other topic yet. It is obvious these two things must be settled for him and he must be made to feel secure and safe again. The practitioner has a decision to make here—whether to put Jack's needs and priorities first or Mandy's. In my experience, the more comfortable and at ease we can make the animal as we begin our communication, the more effectively we can then work through the problems that exist. I go back to Jack.

L: *Mandy will start working with your motion sickness more* (and I show him pictures of things she will be doing and giving him to help). *But do you understand now about why she is taking you around so much?*

J: (He guesses so. He can't separate it all out still, or the sickness part of it. It all just kind of blurs together so is not a real pleasant thing for him.)

L: *I totally understand. And we will certainly work with that. We are so glad you told us. Mandy will start giving you something for that* *before you leave each time, and she will also tell you what to expect each day she takes you with her.*

J: *How often?*

L: *I'll ask her. But do you understand what I just told you? That she will let you know where you are going each time?*

J: (Yes, and he likes that.)

L: (After a quick check with Mandy) *Once or twice a week? How does that sound?*

J: (He's a little hesitant and slow in responding, and I can still sense his anxiety about it.)

INSIGHTS: *I quickly put Jack on "hold" again and recommend that Mandy start with only once a week, adding whatever remedies she thinks appropriate to control the motion sickness, in order to get Jack more comfortable with the trailer again. I do this in order to really pin it down and give Jack an absolute as to what to expect about the frequency of his trailer rides. It is very important not to leave him hanging about this, especially because he is so anxious about it.*

Closure is as important for our animal companions as it is for us. You want to leave the session being able to actually feel a sense of relief and understanding in both the animal and your client. Choosing a specific course of action that can be described to the animal is usually very helpful.

L: (I went back to Jack and let him know that trailering would resume, but just one time per week, with great attention to and care for the motion sickness, and would progress from there, depending on how things went. I reiterated that Mandy would keep him apprised as to where they were going and when.)

J: (This relieved Jack greatly. I could "hear" a nice big sigh and feel a sensation of relaxation in Jack, which I felt in my own body.)

INSIGHTS: This feeling of ease or relief is what you wait for when resolving a difficult topic. Once you feel it, you can generally move on to other questions or topics. However, if there is no comfortable resolution yet to be had, the animal's emotional state may preclude going forward in any meaningful or effective way. In this case, at this point we had finished covering Jack's main concerns and were able to leave him feeling good about them. So we could then begin delving into the more urgent matter at hand—the bucking incident.

Segueing from topic to topic within a communication should be done naturally and in rhythm with all the factors that might come into play. Emotional tone in particular, i.e. feelings of acceptance, relief, excitement, are all indicators of when you can move on to a new topic. In this case we achieved real understanding and relief on Jack's part so I felt he was finally up to taking a look at the rest of the agenda.

If, on the other hand, he had been so preoccupied and stressed out from his nausea and anxiety about trailering that he couldn't concentrate on anything else, we would have continued until we achieved relief on that topic and perhaps would have tabled the next topic for a few days. In this instance, on we go.

L: *Why were you afraid of the trailer that day?* (I showed him in pictures what I meant, and when, and kept this question very general.)

J: (He just didn't want to go out in the trailer again. Plus he was kind of worked up anyway right then, or his nervous system was.)

L: *Yes, Mandy thought you were. Do you know what happened that day?*

INSIGHTS: *I was referring to the buck-off here, and I showed Jack a picture as I asked the question. In order not to "lead" him with the picture or put any ideas in his head that weren't his own, the picture I chose to show him was the one he probably saw when he turned around and saw Mandy on the ground. I did not want to assume he <u>knew</u> he had bucked her off, so I did not want to put the suggestion in his head through a picture of that happening.*

J: (He did not. He was in a total quandary about it when I broached the idea of Mandy's going off of him! He showed me, rather than actually said, *"It's like one minute I was there,"* and then *"The next minute she was gone!"* I could tell from his tone that he was as surprised and dismayed as she was, and the way he conveyed this all to me was very humorous because he was so shocked by it.)

L: *Jack, thank you. I understand.*

INSIGHTS: *Here I put Jack on hold again and took a moment to tell Mandy exactly what Jack's view was of the bucking incident. It was short and sweet, he knew nothing about what had happened, or that he had anything to do with her being on the ground. For that reason we left the topic quickly and did not belabor it or emphasize it in any way.*

We did not address point number five at all (letting him know that it was not appropriate under any circumstances to buck her off). Doing so would have been planting the seed or idea in his head that he actually might be able to do such a thing—something he himself had not yet conceived of. (In this case, Jack's bucking was a product of instinctive behavior. Bucking to get rid of an irritant is natural behavior for an equine. Jack's bucking was due to the fact that an acute irritant, Mandy's spur, had roused him from a near somnolent state, so his reaction was purely instinctive and had nothing to do with trying to get Mandy off his back.) We also did not ask him about whether he was affected by the hay, point number four. He had already made it clear to us that his nervous system was affected by something that day. Mandy felt she did not need more information from him on this point, and he might not have made a connection anyway.

L: *Jack, all of this stuff Mandy is doing is just to keep you working toward doing really fun things together in your life. Going to more clinics, more rides, etc. How did you like the last clinic* (I show him mental pictures—it had been a three-day training workshop)?

J: (He shows me that, after he figured it out he enjoyed it, but it seemed to take quite a while—many hours [the whole first day, Mandy later confirmed]. From this I could tell it took Jack some period of time to know why he was doing something. He needed to know why he was doing things. He didn't do them just for joie de vivre, like some horses or mules. He needed to have a purpose and a reason to do things.)

L: (I told Jack that he was doing wonderfully well with his work, and that Mandy was very proud of him. I reminded him that she was not going to take him away somewhere and that she would talk to him about their trailer rides and would take care of his nausea. I thanked him for talking to us and signed off with him.)

INSIGHTS: The most important thing Mandy and I learned in this particular communication was that Jack was prone to suddenly "disconnect" or "space out" while he was working. This happened when he got bored or lulled by too little stimulation or contact, or inadequate cues or signals. A spaced-out equine, as any horse or mule owner can tell you, is a loaded cannon! When Mandy touched her spur to Jack's side while he was in this condition, it was as if a bee had stung him, and he reacted accordingly. He had momentarily *forgotten that she was even on his back. Interestingly, Mandy made a point of stating that she is the same way and can easily lose focus and tune out in her life. This session, therefore, was a good lesson for her, in that she learned she must pay attention, stay fully present, and feel for when Jack was disconnecting or when she herself might be. An animal communicator's job is to facilitate understanding between species of all kinds, and frequently life lessons come through during what may seem like simple cases. Usually, the human involved will see and accept the lesson wholeheartedly, often even having a huge "Aha" moment in their own personal growth that nothing else could have provided so effectively. This is just one of the wonderful bonuses of this work, and this session with Jack and Mandy are a case in point!*

(Please note: A telephone or in-person session gives the practitioner the luxury of going back and forth between the animal and human at the time of the consult, as reflected in this case when Jack is put on "hold" in order to get information from Mandy. An equally effective conversation can be had, however, when that is not an option, as one can always go back to an animal after the session is over and "fill in the blanks," if specific information needs to be clarified.)

CHAPTER FOURTEEN

THE STORY OF RUBY AND HER FILLY, SAVING GRACE

MIRACLES REALLY DO HAPPEN

I hope the examples, stories, and explanations in this book have given you a glimpse of the broad, deep, and mystical world of the animal kingdom. Communication with animals is a wonderful, inspiring, and soul-nourishing way to connect with other beings and with ourselves. I leave you now with a story of grace and miracles which I hope will keep you inspired should you decide to walk the path of animal communication at any level. Real communication, between any species, is a bond that brings us all toward the oneness we are striving for. Enjoy!

Many years ago I was asked by a holistic equine veterinarian and her client, Debbie, to communicate with one of Debbie's brood mares, Ruby, a twelve-year-old Thoroughbred mare. This was in early April of 1999. Ruby had been delivered of a healthy foal on April 1. I say "delivered of" because the birth was grueling for Ruby—she came close to dying.

Ruby was a large, gleaming chestnut with a brilliant show jumping career behind her who had come to Debbie just a few months before. Debbie didn't really know much about her, just that she had superb bloodlines which, when blended with Debbie's stallion, would produce fabulous jumpers.

After the birth, Ruby was so traumatized and exhausted she could not stay on her feet for the first several days. She was also extremely depressed and seemed to have lost the will to live. Debbie and her vet wanted to know what was going on and why she wasn't coming around, and that's why they called me. Fortunately Ruby's baby was large and thriving with an indomitable spirit, a spunky "grulla" (steel grey) with the sign of the cross over her back like many burros and native equines have. She was quickly dubbed "Saving Grace" by the family because of her miraculous survival. Grace was apparently unaffected by her birth trauma and even learned to nurse with her mother lying down! In fact, the great spirit Grace inherited from Ruby can be seen in a video Debbie now owns of Ruby at the height of her career, taking the jumps with great exuberance and skill and obviously very excited about her work. Where was that spirit now?

As Ruby's due date got closer, she began going downhill physically and emotionally. Her feet swelled and became painful and she spent an increasing amount of time lying down. She was depressed and lethargic. Homeopathic treatment was started, but not much progress could be made because of Ruby's emotional state. Ruby was also on super-food supplements to make sure she was receiving complete nutritional support.

Debbie's small private breeding farm provided the best of the best in every way for all her horses, so Ruby's care was exceptional.

When labor began it was difficult and unproductive. After several hours, Dr. Ward, the veterinarian, was called and upon palpating Ruby, discovered that little Gracie was presenting in a position that is impossible to deliver. Her nose was down and pointed in the right direction to enter the world, but her front legs were back along her body instead of tucked up under her chin where they should have been. Normally a veterinarian can correct such a situation by simply reaching into the birth canal and pulling the legs into position. Dr. Ward is a petite woman however, and Ruby was quite a large mare, so Dr. Ward was unable reach the foal's legs. Meanwhile, Ruby was down and in a dangerous state of distress, and things were getting worse by the hour.

To add to the challenges presented by Ruby's labor, a tumultuous early spring storm was underway with lightning and thunder and gale force winds. In spite of this, there was nothing to do but get Ruby to a clinic as fast as possible. Somehow Dr. Ward and Debbie got Ruby up and loaded into a trailer and over to the largest equine hospital in Texas, an hour away. Debbie drove through the storm, hell-bent-for-leather, and Dr. Ward rode in the trailer with Ruby, the entire way doing acupressure work on the baby's nose, which was all she could reach inside Ruby.

Once they got to the hospital, it took *six* men to save Grace and Ruby!

About a week after the birth I went to visit Ruby. She was standing at the back of her stall with her head down in the corner. As soon as I walked up she came over to me and seemed eager to communicate, as if she had been expecting me. Meanwhile, Gracie was sashaying and hopping around all over the place, inviting her mother to join her in the joy of life, but Ruby's depression was apparent in every fiber of her being. She was also really angry, and that was the very first emotion/communication that hit me—like a brick it was so strong!

I was shocked, but stayed still and open to see what would come next. Ruby couldn't really tell me why she was so mad at first, but it was obvious her hostility was directed toward the world in general and everyone in it. It was interesting to me that she wanted to talk in spite of this. Unable to get much information from her at first, I started telling her how much Debbie loved her and how glad she was to have Ruby, how she planned to keep her at the farm forever, and how upset everyone was over Ruby's obvious suffering and poor condition. I let her know how much we all wanted to help her and asked her if there was anything she could tell us that might help.

Ruby finally started letting go of her hostile façade and, as she softened, I could feel a great despair within her. She then began showing me pictures along with vague ideas and impressions about something that had happened to her in her past. It was a short but shocking story.

Ruby showed me that her only previous foal had been taken from her way too early, and she had never seen it again. This was her first baby, and she loved it with all her heart. The picture I saw was of a very young foal just a few weeks of age, far too young to be weaned. Ruby had been plunged into a lengthy period of grief and despair as well as great physical imbalance and distress. That was all she showed me. Her sadness was so great and her heart so heavy over this that I started crying as I tried to relate the story to Debbie.

All I could do was reassure Ruby over and over again that such an incident would never ever happen with Debbie. I also told her that Grace was in perfect health and there was no reason for worry, and that Debbie was going to raise and show her, so there would be plenty of time for a normal, timely weaning. Ruby visibly relaxed and began releasing a great weight from her soul. Before we left, I thanked her and told her how honored I felt that she would open up to me in this way.

Now that Dr. Ward knew there was such a huge grief inside Ruby's heart, she was able to treat her for it with the homeopathic remedy Ignatia, named for St. Ignatius, which is wonderfully healing for shock and heartache. After that, and with Ruby's new understanding of what her future held, the other constitutional remedies Dr. Ward was using started taking effect. Ruby began getting better by the day and grew much, much happier.

Meanwhile, unbeknownst to me, Debbie called the sales agent through whom she had purchased Ruby. She asked him to check out Ruby's history and to find out what had happened at her previous home. He called her back and this is what he reported. Ruby's previous and only foal had developed a condition known as "joint ill" at four weeks of age. Treatment was delayed to the point where the baby was finally taken from her mother shortly thereafter, put in a station wagon, and transported to a veterinary clinic where she died soon after arrival. Ruby was turned out to pasture and left on her own to deal with her painfully engorged udder and her confusion and grief. She was ill for months and was never her brilliant self again.

Once we learned about this, we went back to Ruby and explained to her what had happened—that her baby had been very sick and could not be made well. We told her how sorry we were that she had had to go through such a tragic time, and that we understood her much better now. We apologized for the fact that sometimes humans, in their ignorance and unawareness of the needs of other species, can gravely mishandle situations and often do not understand the repercussions. We thanked her for sharing her story with us and for being such a strong and noble being.

Ruby continued to strengthen over time. The traumas she had undergone were very deleterious for such a large horse, and they did leave their mark. She will always need special care and supplements. But soon after our communication session and Dr. Ward's wonderful help, she began acting like a normal horse mama, enjoying life with her baby, and expending a lot of energy keeping that little one in line! In the following months Debbie would take her out on easy bareback jaunts, where Ruby was visibly proud and excited. She received very special attention and her every need was catered to. Later, after Grace was weaned, Ruby could be seen prancing and trotting in the pasture, where she was queen of the small broodmare band.

Oh! Saving Grace was moved to a nearby pasture with other youngsters and was carefully trained and groomed for her own show career. She became large and sturdy and, as always, had no fear—a great asset in a jumper. In fact, she has a scar on her nose from jumping a fence to get to her mama during her weaning. And although her color darkened as she grew older, you could still see the sign of the cross on her back—there to keep us reminded that miracles really do happen.

Leta Worthington literally "lives, eats, and breathes" animals at her home near Santa Fe, New Mexico – where she also teaches, consults, and writes about animal communication... with lots of help!

For more information visit Leta's Web site:
www.herbsandanimals.com

And her blog, *A Day in the Life... of an Animal Communicator:*
http://herbsandanimals.wordpress.com

Made in the USA
San Bernardino, CA
19 October 2013